# FOUNDATIONS OF THE
# MODERN WORLD

# FOUNDATIO

# MODERN

# WORLD

*Cambridge: At the University Press, 1963*

# NS OF THE

*by* JOHN FERGUSON

*Professor of Classics, University College, Ibadan*

PUBLISHED BY

THE SYNDICS OF THE CAMBRIDGE UNIVERSITY PRESS

Bentley House, 200 Euston Road, London, N.W. 1
American Branch: 32 East 57th Street, New York 22, N.Y.
West African Office: P.O. Box 33, Ibadan, Nigeria

©

CAMBRIDGE UNIVERSITY PRESS

1963

*Printed in Great Britain by Jarrold and Sons Ltd, Norwich*

# PREFACE

IN addition to the original authorities I have made wide use of modern treatments of the ancient world. Detailed acknowledgment would not be appropriate; enough to mention that the *Cambridge Ancient History* and *Cambridge Medieval History* have been invaluable. In addition I owe much to the memory of a scholar and teacher of genius, the Rev. M. P. Charlesworth, whose premature death was a grievous loss to the world of historical scholarship and to life at Cambridge.

I would wish to express my gratitude to the Cambridge University Press for the invitation to undertake this work and their encouragement through it; to my secretary, Mrs Lewis, for wrestling successfully with my illegibilities; to my friend and colleague, Mr Victor Prescott, now of the University of Melbourne, for the maps which so greatly enhance the book. A number of friends have read the book in manuscript, and it has gained much from their correction of fact, challenge to opinion and removal of obscurity or verbosity; needless to say, they are not responsible for defects which remain. They are Miss Winifred Ayanru, Mr Patrick Considine, Mr Ola Esan, Mr Harold Guite, Mr Arthur Hands, Mr George Jackson, Miss Juliet Udezue, and, last but not least, my wife.

J. F.

IBADAN

*For*

FRANK AND BEATRICE

# CONTENTS

| | | |
|---|---|---|
| I | BEGINNINGS | *page* I |
| 2 | THE JEWS | 17 |
| 3 | THE GREEKS | 30 |
| 4 | THE HELLENISTIC AGE | 52 |
| 5 | ROME | 64 |
| 6 | CHRISTIANITY | 85 |
| 7 | BYZANTIUM | 103 |
| 8 | ISLAM | 115 |
| 9 | THE MIDDLE AGES | 128 |
| 10 | THE RENAISSANCE AND REFORMATION | 154 |
| 11 | THE PAST IN THE PRESENT | 172 |
| | *For further reading* | 182 |
| | *Acknowledgments* | 184 |

# I

# BEGINNINGS

## BEFORE MAN

IN the beginning, more than three thousand million years ago, it seems that the sun had an immense star with it. That star burst in a series of explosions. Gas from these explosions began to whirl round the sun, and from this gas were formed the planets. On one of these, the earth, life emerged; how, we do not know. Animal life may have started more than two thousand million years ago. The simplest form of living matter is called protoplasm. Probably the first living bodies consisted of single cells. Gradually more complex creatures emerged, perhaps in the sea. From fish came reptiles, coming out on to the dry land, from reptiles birds in the air and mammals on the ground. The story of the development of life is the story of evolution.

## MAN

No one knows for certain when or where man first appeared on the earth. Probably all men have a common ancestry, deriving from more primitive animals by a series of jumps in the process of change by evolution, called mutations. We may suppose these significant changes to have taken place about half a million years ago—not more than a million. It is likely that the scene of the changes was East Africa, though some people have argued for the Caucasus, and others, less convincingly, have supposed that the changes took place in a number of different parts of the world at the same time.

Man differs from most animals in the fact that he stands upright. This has enabled him to support a larger brain and develop a more flexible hand. From quite early stages we can trace qualities in man which the other animals do

A Stone Age flint hand axe, found in the gravel beds of the Thames valley in England. These axes, carefully formed by chipping or flaking with a wood instrument, were secured to a wooden handle, probably with leather thongs.

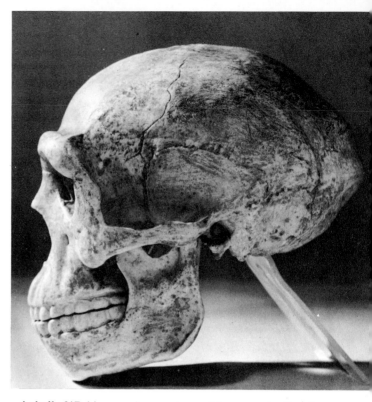

A skull of 'Peking man', reconstructed from remains found at Choukoutien, near Peking. The earliest forms of man are classified into three groups. The *Australopithecinae* were the earliest, and evolved perhaps 1,000,000 years ago. They walked erect or partly erect, but had very small brains— about the size of an ape's. The second group, the *Pithecanthropiae*, emerged more than 100,000 years ago. Peking man (*c.* 400,000 B.C.) belongs to this group. The brain is larger, half-way between an ape's and modern man's in size; but the forehead is flattened and low, with heavy eyebrow ridges, and the lower part of the face juts forward. Peking man had primitive stone-chopping and scraping tools, used fire, and lived on animal—and possibly human—flesh, obtained by hunting and trapping. This involved teamwork and therefore speech.

This early period saw great climatic changes, in particular the advance and withdrawal of great ice-sheets. In these conditions man evolved, and so did human society. At last *Homo sapiens*, fully erect, with slender limbs and a large brain, emerged, perhaps in Western Asia, and spread over the greater part of the earth.

not possess. Man controls his surroundings. This he succeeds in doing by the use of tools, devised by his superior brain and used by his flexible hand. The cat uses its paws for fighting, the rabbit for burrowing; man fits a sword

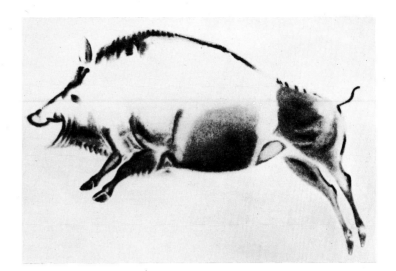

A painting of a boar, from the rock-paintings in the caves of Altamira in Spain. These very skilful and colourful paintings were made far from the surface of the earth and the light of day. It is thought that their purpose was magical.

or a spade on to his hand and can do both; later still he devises the atom bomb and the bulldozer.

Man seems to acquire a sense of values which are scarcely to be seen in other animals. Primitive man is an artist. His art may be magical in purpose; he may be seeking to master the animal he represents by the act of representing it. But when we look at the boar painted by some primitive worker at Altamira in Spain, the swimming deer of the Lascaux caves in France or some of the rock-paintings of the Fezzan in North Africa, we feel that there is something in the work which goes beyond its practical purpose, art as well as magic.

Man shows from the first a belief in something beyond nature. He buries his dead with food and drink and weapons and fire nearby, expecting that there is a life beyond death in which the dead man will need these things. He rubs his spear against a spear which has hunted well, for this last has power, *mana* as it is usually called, and this power may be transferred. He makes thundering noises to bring on rain and jumps to make his crops grow. But alongside this he worships; even 'low races' have 'high gods'. Religion comes early into the picture.

Further, in historical times we can see that man is intellectually and morally different from other animals. He alone has made for himself a philosophy and an ethic; that he often falls below the moral standard he himself sets is another story. Man is reflective; he asks questions about the world and about his own behaviour in a way no other animal does. Whether these qualities go right back to the beginnings of man, whether, that is to say, they

3

are a biological feature of *Homo sapiens*, or whether they have emerged in the course of man's own growth and development, we have no means of knowing. Suffice to say that they are distinctive of human beings.

## THE AGES OF MAN

We cannot know much about individual men of early times; it is writing which enables us to meet, as it were, individuals out of the past, and for a long time man could not write. So we judge humans from the past by their culture, by the way they lived. The old division used to be between the Stone Age, the Bronze Age and the Iron Age; the names show the chief material from which men made their tools. Modern students use a more complicated scheme, on which they are not fully agreed themselves; the most important of the early stages are the Palaeolithic or Old Stone Age, the Neolithic or New Stone Age, and Palaeometallic or Old Metal Age. Throughout the world most peoples have gone through these stages. But the development has been at a very different rate in different parts; as V. Gordon Childe pointed out, the Neolithic Stage ended before 3000 B.C. in Egypt, in New Zealand only after A.D. 1800!

As we have written records in any part of the world from only about 3000 B.C., we are left with a long period with no accurate date. Sometimes the remains, pottery or implements or burials or whatever it may be, can be related to the great changes of the earth's surface associated with the Ice Ages. More recently it has proved possible to date some remains by measuring their carbon content, one part of which decays at a known rate.

We have very few skeletons of really early man, which suggests that the human being was a rare animal. During the Old Stone (Palaeolithic) period he devised tools: in Africa and western Europe by shaping a lump of stone for use, in the centre of the great land mass of Europe and Asia by using flakes knocked off a lump of stone. He lived by hunting animals, fishing, and gathering roots and berries. There are some signs of primitive trade. There were certainly magic rites to help the food-supply, and paintings which are admired as art today.

The New Stone (Neolithic) period shows an important change. Instead of collecting food which had grown naturally, man began to grow food himself.

4

Childe described the period well, as it appeared in Europe. 'It is represented by farmers who cultivate cereals, leguminous plants and flax, and breed sheep, goats, cattle and pigs, who live in commodious well-built houses, grouped in villages, and who are equipped with efficient axes or adzes, edged by polishing, and have mastered the arts of converting clay into pottery and of spinning and weaving.' The polished stone axe generally belongs to this period and is often taken as a sign of it.

The Old Metal (Palaeometallic) Age shows another great change. Man learned to work copper—and to mix it with tin to make bronze. In the great river-valleys of Mesopotamia and Egypt it was possible to grow plenty of grain and transport it by water for storage. Hence food-producers were freed to work in metal. Other changes followed. The wheel was invented, perhaps the greatest single step forward in human history. This improved the making of pottery and made transport easier; and the sailing-ship further improved transport. Trade grew, and men began to live in towns instead of villages. These changes lead us to the edge of historical times in Europe and the Near East.


## RACE AND LANGUAGE

Men are different from one another, and may be grouped according to a broad division which is based upon the nature of their hair, colour of skin, shape of head and similar factors. Such groups are called races. Thus the races of Europe—Nordic, 'Alpine' (found also in western and central Asia), and 'Mediterranean' (found also in the Middle East, East Africa and southern Asia)—have hair not essentially different from that of the ape, wavy with an elliptical cross-section, whereas the Negro race of Africa has tightly curled hair, each hair showing a flat cross-section, and the Mongol race of Asia has straight hair with a circular cross-section. Racial differences are strictly physical, and no race can claim to be intellectually or morally better than another. There are wide physical differences within each race: the Negroes include some of the tallest and some of the smallest men in the world.

Men are sometimes divided by language-families. Modern languages are often related to one another, perhaps through a common ancestor, as French, Italian, Spanish, Portuguese, Rumanian, and to some extent English, derive from Latin. This whole family, which includes Greek and Sanskrit, is called Indo-European, because it is found in India and Europe. Another language-family is Bantu, which is widely spread in Africa.

## EARLY SOCIETY

Man is a social animal; he tends to live with others. The simplest unit of society is the family. But the family is a loose unit. In some societies the mother looks after the children while the father goes off; in such societies woman is much more powerful. The children when old enough may leave. Sometimes the mother will have several husbands; sometimes the father several wives. A more complicated unit is the clan or sib, a group related to one another either on the mother's side or the father's side, but (unless the mother and father are from the same clan) not both. A boy may belong to the same clan as his mother's brother or his father's brother in different societies. More complicated still is the tribe, a group of people who live together in a given area as a unity. A tribe may arise out of a clan, but it need not do so.

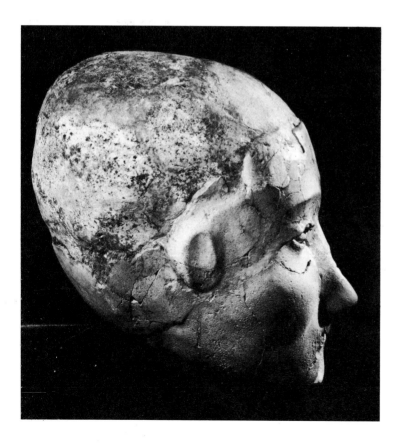

Skull of a Proto-Neolithic man from Jericho with the face modelled in clay (*c.* 6000 B.C.).

The site of ancient Jericho was occupied f thousands of years: first by hunter-fishers wl lived in small groups, perhaps in caves, an may have harvested a little grain. Later the were larger settlements; these used grain muc more, built huts of mud brick inside defensi walls, and may have kept domesticated goat Later still, rectangular houses with plast floors were built round courtyards; and fro this period this skull comes. It shows advance in religious practice, to be seen in tl treatment of the dead. At Jericho the earlie settlers had separated the head, perhaps as tl house of the spirit. Now the skull was giv a face; and a very individual face, with the ey inlaid with shell and the features fine modelled. It seems as if the memory of individual, a *person*, was being perpetuated.

Of particular interest are those tribes or clans which are associated with an animal (or, less often, a plant) with which they identify themselves; such an animal is called a totem. Members of such a totem-clan believe that the animal is their ancestor and can give them strength; they respect it and are forbidden to eat it except at special ceremonies. Here is a strong tie holding the tribe or clan together. Whatever the system, man has a strong gregarious instinct; he tends to group together; and our complex modern societies have evolved from such simple groupings.

## CIVILIZATIONS

If we except India, the Far East, and Central America, the civilizations of the rest of the world hold together in a complicated but coherent story. To put it differently—again excepting India, the Far East, and Central America—three significant strands from the past have gone to the making of the modern world. They come from Athens, Rome and Jerusalem. From Athens, through Rome, Byzantium and Islam, has come our intellectual and artistic heritage. Rome has given us practical achievement, especially in government and law. Jerusalem, through Judaism, Christianity and Islam, has been the cradle of religion. These facts remain true in New York or Moscow, in Lagos or Johannesburg, and this book tries to show something of the past which still lives in the present. But Athens, Rome and Jerusalem also had their past, and we must begin by glancing at those areas, within reach of the eastern Mediterranean, in which civilization first arose.

## EGYPT

The first developments of civilization are associated with the Nile valley. There, already before 4000 B.C., it seems that there was trading in copper, and sufficient ability in engineering to alter the course of the Nile. The years after 4000 saw an increase in travel and trade, a blossoming of culture, including the development of writing, and the building of the first pyramids, those curious-shaped tombs which the ruler set his people to build during the

An aerial photograph of the pyramids at Gizeh. The pyramids are enormous tombs. The ancient Egyptians were much pre-occupied with life after death. They believed that the spirit survived if the body was preserved and provided with all its needs in the after-life. Tombs became more elaborate and richly furnished, and then huge conical structures were built over the underground tomb chambers. The Great Pyramid built for Cheops and his queen is 756 feet square at the base, rose to 481 feet, and incorporated 2,300,000 blocks of stone each weighing $2\frac{1}{2}$ tons; and it probably took 100,000 forced labourers working in spells of three months each, and 4000 masons and permanent labourers, 20 years to build it. Over twenty pyramids were built during the Old Kingdom alone; so one can imagine the driving force of the religious idea, and the power and status of the pharaohs.

months when the Nile floods over the land and the farmers are unemployed. But too much depended on the ruler or pharaoh. Things fell apart; then there was a revival after the year 3000 B.C., and a period of military expansion to the south, and some magnificent engineering feats in the building of dams and canals. Then follows another period of darkness and indeed domination by foreign monarchs, until the establishment of the New Kingdom about 1738 B.C. saw Egyptian civilization in all its splendour. The wheeled chariot came to Egypt from Asia and enabled the Egyptians to extend their conquests to Syria and the coastal plain of Palestine. There were two centuries of imperial grandeur. Thothmes III (early fifteenth century B.C.) was the great conqueror, but a statesman too and humane in his treatment of his subjects. His courtiers called him 'true of voice', 'splendid in valour, in might and in triumph', a 'young bull, ready with its horns, irresistible', 'a circling comet which shoots out flames and gives forth its substance in fire'. Amonhotep III (c. 1400 B.C.), his grandson, was the great peace-time ruler, who encouraged

The colossal statues of kings, forty feet high, carved in the solid rock of Abu Simbel, by the Nile. This is the funerary temple of Rameses II; behind the statues the halls of the temple tunnel into the rock.

every art, from the making of glass beads to the mighty temple at Luxor. With his son, Amonhotep IV (*c.* 1370 B.C.), who changed his name to Aken-Aten (Ikhnaten), 'Aten's servant', the dynasty decays. Ikhnaten was a religious reformer who believed in one god, whom he identified with the sun. But he was an unbusinesslike ruler, and though the riches that remained are seen in the stupendous wealth of the tomb of Tut-ankh-Amon, and Rameses II (thirteenth century B.C.) in his sixty-four years as ruler built more than any who had gone before, Egypt never quite reached the same point of glory again.

When we think of Egypt we think of the pyramids and the massive temples, and the material remains of the civilization are certainly very impressive. Or

A page of a copy of 'The Book of the Dead' about 1300 B.C. These books were buried, with much else, in Egyptian tombs to provide for the needs of the dead. They contained hymns and prayers for their eternal happiness. The illustration shows a funeral scene. The mummified body, in the mummy-case, is held at the edge of the tomb by a dog-headed god. Women and servants perform farewell rites. Note the hieroglyphic writing, which reads vertically. The book is written on papyrus, made of thin strips of the pith of the papyrus plant. One layer of strips was laid vertically, another horizontally, and the two were glued together.

we think of their belief in a life after death, which can be seen in many of the tombs and in a remarkable volume called *The Book of the Dead* which deals with the fate of the soul after death. But the greatest contribution of Egypt did not lie here. The Egyptians noticed in quite early times that the Nile flooded (with the melting of snow in the mountains far to the south) on the average once every 365 days, and divided time into years of 365 days. Of course, this was not quite exact; there was an error of six hours, which became serious as the years passed. But in this calculation we have the direct ancestor of the modern calendar.

## MESOPOTAMIA

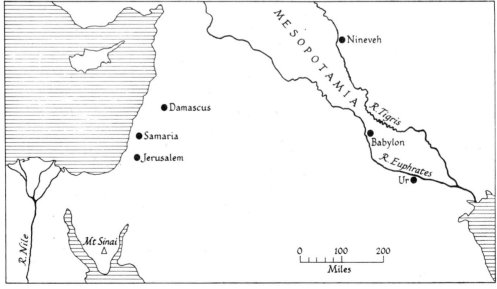

The cradle of civilization.

Mesopotamia means 'the land between the rivers'; it is the country which lies to the north of the Persian Gulf, watered by the Tigris and Euphrates. Today it is a land of desert mingled with marshland; in old times its prosperity depended on irrigation.

The first people to establish civilization there were the Sumerians in the south and the Akkadians (a Semitic people) in the north. We do not know where they came from; perhaps north-west India, perhaps the Caspian. They reached a high level of culture. They built mighty temples called *ziggurats*,

The great *ziggurat* of Ur-Nammu. A *ziggurat* is a massive stepped platform, bearing a temple on the highest stage. The Ubaid people who lived at Ur and other centres in Mesopotamia built towns of kiln-baked brick set in bitumen. The size of the *ziggurat* suggests a highly organized society and an advanced religious system. Indeed city life seems to have been centred on the temple and its priests. The approach up the stepped ramp to the holy place of mystery, worship and sacrifice at the top is well calculated to produce a sense of awe.

towering by stages towards the sky; the biblical story of the Tower of Babel is a memory of one of these. They used arches in building, unknown in Europe before about 300 B.C. Like the Egyptians, they could write. They could calculate accurately the length of time it would take a sum of money to double itself at 20 per cent compound interest. Using the *ziggurats* as observatories they made detailed observations of the stars. The height of this early culture may be placed between 3000 and 2000 B.C., and Sir Leonard Woolley remarked that in achievement alone Sumer must rank high in human history, and in influence yet higher, for Sumer provided the roots from which later civilization grew.

From the end of this period and the continuing prosperity which followed two names stand out. Sargon I (perhaps in the 2300s B.C.) lived in memory as a military leader; he used the new secret weapon, the war-chariot, in making Sumer and Akkad into one kingdom, developed trade and secured a stock of precious metals, especially silver. More interesting, because more constructive, is Hammurabi. The centre of power had shifted to Babylon. Hammurabi was a skilled soldier and diplomat. But he lives for us because of his legal code. A great ruler, he stands as a high point in the history of the rule of law. His code is remarkable for its breadth. We may notice the careful

The stele, or pillar, of Hammurabi. At the top Hammurabi stands in an attitude of worship before the sun-god. Below, the legal code is inscribed in cuneiform script.

A Sumerian statue of early dynastic times (3200–2800 B.C.) found beside an altar at Tell Asmar, in Mesopotamia.

The statue, made of yellow limestone with inlaid shell eyes, is one of several. The figures seem to be bearing an offering of liquid to be poured out as a libation to the god. Some of the statues bear inscriptions, such as 'It offers prayers', or 'Statue, say to my king...'. So the statue was placed in the temple by a worshipper, whom it may resemble, as a representation of himself; a kind of permanent ambassador to the god.

regulation of family life, the sympathy for debtors, and the protection of the person against violence and wrong. The punishments sometimes seem to us crude; for example, if a patient dies under an operation, the surgeon's offending hand is cut off. But it was an advance on anything known before, and in its treatment of women—the married woman has equal rights with her husband and can own her own property—and its care for industrial workers, is in advance of anything known in Europe for thousands of years. We cannot date Hammurabi precisely: he lived probably some time after 2000 B.C.

## THE HITTITES

Recently attention has been drawn to the culture of the Hittites who lived in the high table-land to the north of Asia Minor and were responsible for the temporary eclipse of Babylon about 1600 B.C. They reached their highest power in the fourteenth century under a king named Suppiluliumas, whose fame was enough for the widowed queen of Egypt to ask for his son in marriage; the boy was murdered on the way and nothing came of it. The Hittites were an agricultural people, but they developed metal-working in silver, copper and, later, iron. They made no great contributions to literature, art, or religion. Their ruling-class had some genius in war, political organization and the administration of justice.

# THE MINOAN CIVILIZATION

Another important civilization, which was unknown before 1900 and discovered by the brilliant work of Sir Arthur Evans, centred on the island of Crete. It is called the Minoan civilization, after the legendary king Minos. The greatest glory of this culture belongs to the period 2000–1400 B.C., after which it went into a rapid decline. In its prosperity mighty palaces were built, of which that at Knossos is best known, a labyrinth of a place covering five acres in all. The palace was equipped with bathrooms and efficient drainage. Exquisite paintings adorned the walls; one shows a Cretan officer commanding Negro troops, another dolphins swimming, another a monkey gathering saffron. The storerooms, which are extensive, were carefully checked, and detailed accounts were kept. The Cretans were a religious people and worshipped a goddess who represents the power of nature and is often shown with animals; the symbol of a double axe is common, but we cannot be certain what it meant. They were also a sporting people and loved to watch acrobats catching the horns of bulls and leaping on to their backs, a difficult and dangerous feat. But the most important fact about Minoan prosperity is that it depended on sea-power. The towns were not even protected by walls, and there must have been a considerable trade with Egypt and elsewhere.

The throne room of the palace of Minos at Knossos in Crete, c. 2000 B.C. The wall-paintings have been restored.

# WRITING

The exact origin of writing is lost in the dim past. Man early learned to make a mark on a stone or a notch on a stick to remind himself or someone else of something he wanted done. Such a mark might well take the form of a drawing of an animal or some other object. From this it was not a long step to agree that such a drawing, often stylized, should be used as a written word. Chinese script, beautiful but cumbrous, depends upon a multitude of such signs; to learn them all is a heavy task. It is a step forward when signs are used, not for words, but for syllables or parts of words. This may be seen, for example, in the 'hieroglyphs' or 'sacred carvings' of Egypt and 'cuneiform' or 'wedge-shapes' of Mesopotamia (the Mesopotamians wrote on clay, where a stroke tended to broaden out with pressure into a wedge). It may be seen also in the Cretan 'Linear B' script, which has recently been deciphered by a young architect named Michael Ventris. The invention of the alphabet, another step forward, was attributed to the Phoenicians, acting on hints from Egypt. The letters of the alphabet recall a former style—*aleph* א is an ox with its horns, *beth* ב a house, and so on.

KING NAR-MER, wearing the crown of upper Egypt, kills an enemy with a stone-headed mace. Behind the king, a slave bears his sandals.

Nar-mer was one of the First Dynasty of pharaohs, who ruled over the united kingdom of Egypt. This relief was carved on one side of a great stone palette in the old royal capital of Hierakonpolis. The palette contains two early hieroglyphs (by the enemy's head). One shows a fish, *nar*, the other a chisel, *mer*. Thus the name of the King, Nar-mer, is written by ignoring the usual or pictorial sense of the symbols ('fish' and 'chisel') and using them for sound values only (nar-mer)—a major step in the evolution of a phonetic script.

# SUMMARY

We cannot give exact dates for these prehistoric events. But in broad outline we can see them as follows:

| | |
|---|---|
| 4000–3000 B.C. | Growth of civilization in Egypt and Mesopotamia. |
| 3000–2000 B.C. | Height of Sumerian culture in Mesopotamia. |
| | Egyptian expansion and engineering feats. |
| 2000–1400 B.C. | Minoan civilization in Crete. |
| 1750–1200 B.C. | Climax of Egyptian prosperity. |
| | Hittites prominent in Asia Minor. |
| | Mesopotamia in eclipse. |

Already by about the year 1500 B.C. we see that the conditions of civilization have been established, and much has been achieved. Man has learned to master his surroundings by the use of tools. The great revolution by which metal, which is both more flexible and more powerful, is used instead of stone, bone and wood, has taken place. Man has learned to live together in communities, to help his neighbour and to receive help from his neighbour, to give and take, and from this living together has emerged the rule of law. Man has learned to speak, and from learning to speak, after many thousands of years has learned to write. Man has learned something of the value of beauty, and has learned in painting, and music and words, to create beauty for himself. Man has come to regard himself as living in a world in which there are divine powers greater than he. How he developed from this point the rest of this book will show.

## 2

# THE JEWS

## RELIGION

WE have seen that one thing which marks man off from the other animals is his sense of religion. It is extremely difficult to explain exactly what this is; perhaps in its simplest form it is the sense that he is not the most important being in the universe. One great scholar has seen the centre of religion in the awe we feel before that which we call 'holy', a mystery which causes us to tremble and yet attracts us. We shrink before God because of the contrast between his perfection and our imperfection, and yet he draws us to him. To take a religious view of life is to see a power beyond the human, a standard of what is good, and a purpose or direction for ourselves.

## WORLD RELIGIONS

It is a curious fact, and one which has never been adequately explained, that all the great world-religions began in Asia. Hinduism is the chief religion of India; Buddhism arose as a reforming movement within and alongside it. Zoroastrianism, the religion of the Parsees, comes from Persia. At the eastern end of the Mediterranean one small tribe, the Hebrews, or Jews as they were later called, caught and clung on to the vision of one single God. The Jewish religion still exists in the modern world, with some 12,000,000 worshippers. But, besides these, from the Jewish vision sprang the two greatest missionary religions of the world, Christianity, with 500,000,000 adherents, which is the chief religion of Europe and has spread from there to America and to those other parts of the world which Europeans have been able to influence, and Islam (sometimes wrongly called Mohammedanism), with 250,000,000 adherents, which is found in Pakistan, western Asia generally, the East Indies and the northern half of Africa. The Old Testament is a sacred book alike to Jews, Christians and Muslims, but the Christians add to it the New Testament, and the Muslims the Quran.

## THE EARLY HISTORY OF THE HEBREWS

We cannot now trace in detail the early history of the Hebrews. Their own legends recorded how Abraham, the father of the race and the type of faith, emigrated from Mesopotamia to Palestine, and this no doubt reflects an historical movement. Some Hebrew folk-lore is closely similar to stories found among the Babylonians. In particular, the story of the great flood, and the man who built an ark and saved some humans and some animals, is found among the Babylonians as well as in the Old Testament, and Sir Leonard Woolley, digging at Ur in Mesopotamia, discovered clear evidence of a disastrous deluge in that part of the world. It is interesting that the name Abram has actually been found in ancient writings from Mesopotamia.

After a while famine drove some of the Hebrews out of Palestine into the fertile and prosperous land of Egypt. Here for a while they flourished, and settled happily, till there came to the throne of Egypt a ruler who decided to exploit these aliens in the land: this was probably the pharaoh Rameses II (thirteenth century B.C.). Such attacks upon foreigners are an unhappy feature of human history in most lands and at most periods. In this crisis the Hebrews found a great leader in Moses. The Egyptians were weakened by a series of plagues and were unable to prevent the wholesale emigration of their serfs.

## THE COVENANT

Moses was son-in-law to the Kenite Hobab. The Kenites worshipped a God named Yahweh (sometimes called Jehovah), who was associated with the volcanic mountain Sinai. As the Hebrews passed this mountain they resolved to adopt Yahweh as their God, and to be adopted by him as his people. This new relation was established by a solemn covenant. It was an unusual

MOSES: the statue by Michelangelo. The aged prophet is shown as still immensely vigorous physically and mentally. Note the muscular arm, the fiery eyes, the frown, the compressed lips. He is holding the stone tablets, inscribed with the Law, handed to him on Mount Sinai.

Moses was often shown, as here, with horns. This is due to a misunderstanding of the Hebrew text of the Old Testament. When he returned from Mount Sinai, according to the Hebrew, his face shone (Hebrew: *qeren*). St Jerome, translating into Latin, wrote that his face had horns (Hebrew: *qaran*). Hence a long artistic tradition in the representation of the prophet.

MOUNT SINAI. The Sinai peninsula is a rocky triangle between Egypt and Palestine. It is not easy to identify the Biblical Mount Sinai with certainty, but this peak is usually taken to be the site of Moses' encounter with God.

relationship in two ways. First, it was free. Yahweh was not dependent on his people. It often happens that a tribal god is so closely associated with the tribe that if the tribe ceases to exist the god passes into nothingness: so it was with Chemosh, the god of the Moabites, but it was not so with Yahweh. This independence of the god from his people made possible the growth of belief that he was not a tribal god like other tribal gods, but the one god of the whole world. Monolatry, the worship of one god (out of many), could give way to monotheism, the belief that one god only existed.

Secondly, Moses linked the covenant, not merely with ritual, in which much primitive religion consists, but with moral demands. These were the Ten Commandments, a simple but exacting moral code.

1. I am the Lord your God.... You shall have no other gods before me.
2. You shall not make yourself a graven image....
3. You shall not take the name of the Lord your God in vain....
4. Remember the sabbath day, to keep it holy....
5. Honour your father and your mother....
6. You shall not kill.
7. You shall not commit adultery.
8. You shall not steal.
9. You shall not bear false witness against your neighbour.
10. You shall not covet your neighbour's house; you shall not covet your neighbour's wife, or his manservant, or his maidservant, or his ox, or his ass, or anything that is your neighbour's.

Moses, in fostering the worship of Yahweh alone, in inducing the Hebrews to think of themselves as 'the people of Yahweh', and above all in linking religion with this moral code, changed history.

## THE SETTLEMENT AND THE KINGDOM

For forty years the Hebrews led a nomadic life on the fringe of the desert. Moses glimpsed the land in which they were to settle, but no more, and it was left to his successor, Joshua (Jesus is a later form of the same name, which means 'Yahweh is salvation'), to lead the expedition by which the twelve tribal groups who made up the whole people settled in Palestine. For over a century they led a troubled and uncertain existence. The farmers already established in the land worshipped gods of fertility. The Hebrews might easily have been absorbed, but, though some were affected, there remained those whom loyalty to the covenant and a certain proud consciousness of destiny kept apart.

For many years they were overpowered by the Philistines from the coast. Eventually they decided to establish a king, against the judgment of those who thought that they should have no king but Yahweh. This was still an age when kings held office by personal prowess. Saul, the first king, was a

DAVID, by Michelangelo. David is seen
a shepherd youth. Over his shoulder lies t
thong of the sling with which he slew Goliat

dominant soldier; David, his successor (*c.* 1000 B.C.), a combination of soldier
and artist; Solomon, the third in line, a shrewd politician up to a point, whose
policies proved in the end disastrous. Under David the kingdom became
independent and comparatively powerful, with its capital in the fortress-city
of Jerusalem. Under Solomon decay set in; the white ants were gnawing
behind the façade. Solomon built the first temple to Yahweh; he also built
himself a far more magnificent palace. The country was bankrupt, and there
are indications that he sold some of his subjects as slaves to bolster up the
national economy. The discontent reached its peak under his successor, and
the kingdom split disastrously and irrevocably into two, Israel with its
capital at Samaria, and Judah with its centre at Jerusalem.

# THE FIRST GREAT PROPHETS

The two kingdoms, like their immediate neighbours, of whom the most important was Syria, now became pawns in the game of power politics. Away to the south-west Egypt was slumbering in prosperity. To the east lay Mesopotamia, and here first Assyria, a mighty military power with few claims on the memory of later ages, and then the more cultured revived kingdom of Babylon arose. Palestine lay on the Fertile Crescent, a curving sweep of irrigated land in the midst of mountain and desert, the only practicable route connecting the empires. The next centuries are a story of petty tribal wars swamped in the ocean of world war. Appeasement and resistance were both tried; in 722 B.C. Samaria fell to Assyria, and a century later, in 586, Jerusalem was finally conquered by Babylon and her leaders taken into exile.

Yet during this period the religious genius of the Hebrews asserted itself in a succession of men called prophets. The prophet, rightly understood, is not the man who foretells but the man who speaks forth; to the Hebrews he was the man who proclaimed the will of Yahweh. Prophets had been known for centuries. There was Nathan who dared to admonish King David for a crime he had committed, Elijah who likewise defied the monarch of the day in Yahweh's name and became a refugee and a fugitive, and his successor Elisha. Their loyalty sometimes took a bloodthirsty turn, as when Elisha was behind a palace revolution which massacred his religious opponents. The eighth century produced three men greater than these, who made vital contributions to the religious thought of man.

Amos (c. 760 B.C.) was a shepherd from Tekoa. His great contribution was twofold. First, he insisted that religion must find its outcome in political and social behaviour. It was no use the upper classes offering religious sacrifices and at the same time oppressing the poor; Yahweh was more concerned about the oppression than the sacrifices, and Amos proclaimed judgment and doom upon the offenders. Secondly, Amos was the first great universalist; his view was not limited by what affected the Hebrews. When he pronounced the anger of Yahweh with the Moabites for atrocities committed against the Edomites—both non-Hebrew peoples—he pronounced that Yahweh was the god of all peoples. 'Are you not like the Ethiopians to me, O people of Israel? says the Lord. Did I not bring up Israel from the land of Egypt—and the Philistines from Caphtor and the Syrians from Kir?'

Hosea (*c.* 740 B.C.) is the most tender of the prophets. He had an unfaithful wife, yet found that he still loved her, and saw in his experience a parable of Yahweh's dealing with his people—continuing to love them and draw them back to him despite their sin. In another unforgettable image Hosea compared Yahweh with a father teaching his little son to walk. To Hosea God was a God of love.

Isaiah (*c.* 720 B.C.) adds to the picture the holiness of God. In the vision which began his ministry he 'saw the Lord sitting upon a throne, high and lifted up' and his impulse was to despair because he was unworthy of the vision. Yet he had the courage to go, like Amos, and proclaim the need for political righteousness at a time of crisis.

In this proclamation of the universality, the moral demand, the love and holiness of Yahweh, religion is beginning to reach the depths of the human spirit and the height of human experience.

THE PROPHET ISAIAH: one of the series of Hebrew prophets portrayed by Michelangelo on the ceiling of the Sistine Chapel in Rome. All of them suggest, in their features and attitude, gravity and power. Isaiah turns from his reading to listen to the angel of God, who seems to be calling him to action.

A portion of a 'Dead Sea Scroll' of Isaiah. These scrolls were found recently in the caves of desert Judaea. This one is the oldest known complete manuscript of any Biblical book. It has been preserved by the dryness of the desert atmosphere. The importance of this find is that we are now able to check the accuracy of our own Old Testament text against this very early text.

These manuscripts were written in columns on animal skins sewn together to form a long roll. The photograph shows a join between skins, and some insertions written vertically. Hebrew script is written from right to left.

# DEUTERONOMY

Alongside the prophets stood the priests. It was left to the priests to organize the message of the prophets, and ensure that the insights of the prophets became part of the common heritage of the people. The record of this is the book we call Deuteronomy, written probably early in the seventh century and rediscovered in 621 in King Josiah's reign, and made an occasion of national repentance.

Deuteronomy is in many ways a remarkable book. It starts from the premiss that Yahweh is the only god, loving towards his people, terrible towards those who reject him. This leads to a ringing call to worship, centralized at Jerusalem, and to the purifying of the people. From this comes a strong emphasis on education, education in history, ritual and correct social conduct. Social conduct includes improving the condition of slaves (though not abolishing slavery), protecting the rights of women, and helping the poor. It has been said of Deuteronomy that it 'is a book of national religion, but it is withal a book of personal religion and so of universal religion'.

Its acceptance was a rebirth, and it came with violence. There was extermination and bloodshed. The lesson of Hosea was not yet learned: bloodthirstiness still ruled. But it was a step forward, the foundation of all that was to come.

# THE EXILE

The second great wave of prophetic religion belongs to the early sixth century B.C. and is associated with the conquest of Jerusalem by Babylon and the removal of the Jewish leaders into exile for fifty years. Here again three figures stand out.

Jeremiah's career spans the forty years preceding the exile. He was the effective founder of personal religion. He prophesied disaster in the name of Yahweh, rightly, for the policies of the statesmen were disastrous. For years Judah muddled through, and the prophet of gloom was mocked and maltreated. In one tremendous passage we see him standing face to face with his god and remonstrating with him. Yet something drove him on. 'If I say, "I will not mention him, or speak any more in his name", there is in my heart as it were a burning fire shut up in my bones, and I am weary with holding it in, and I cannot.' The old covenant (this is the meaning of the Old Testament) was not enough. A new covenant was needed, and this would be written not on stone tablets or paper but on men's hearts. Religion is a matter of inward disposition, not of outward observance.

Ezekiel belongs to the period of the exile; he was unusual in combining the office of priest and the vocation of prophet. He developed Jeremiah's insights. Jeremiah was the prophet of personal religion; Ezekiel proclaimed personal responsibility. Yahweh according to him held each individual responsible for his acts. So he called the people to national regeneration: a vision of a valley of dry bones became the image of the people dead in sin, but given life by the spirit of God. Above all Ezekiel could not believe in a God who was too small. He had known Yahweh in Jerusalem; he knew him also in Babylon. The greatness of Yahweh runs through Ezekiel's writings.

The finest of the prophets we cannot even name. He also belongs to the Exile, and his work has become attached to the words of Isaiah. For this reason he is sometimes called Deutero-Isaiah, or the second Isaiah. Here is the zenith of monotheism—'I am Yahweh and there is no other'—and a vision of the almightiness of the God to whom 'the inhabitants of the earth are like grasshoppers' recounted in poetry which has never been surpassed. But alongside this are the songs of the suffering servant, in which the prophet seems to suggest that suffering willingly undertaken may make for good, and to assert that death is not the end of human life.

## THE RETURN

Hebrew religion has now reached its climax. In 538 B.C. Cyrus of Persia conquered Babylon, and the Jews were free to return. The return was not easy, and our records of the next centuries are scanty. For 350 years there was no political security, and then only a brief period of independence under a ruling house known as the Maccabees before they finally succumbed to Rome. Meantime in the Diaspora or Dispersion they spread throughout the Mediterranean region. We may, however, trace some significant religious ideas during this period.

First, Jewish religion became the religion of a book, the book of the Law, as recorded in the first five books of the Old Testament. This led to an emphasis on outward observance, for which Jesus of Nazareth criticized his contemporaries.

Secondly, this was a period of expectancy. The Jews were looking forward to the coming of the Messiah, Christ, or Anointed King, who would appear in a cataclysm, purify his people, remove wickedness, and either make subservient or destroy the Gentiles, that is, the non-Jews.

Thirdly, by a paradox this period saw at once a blending of Jewish ideas with foreign elements, and a new exclusiveness. The Greek Hecataeus wrote: 'Under the rule of nations during later times the Jews greatly modified the traditions of their fathers.' We can see this in the introduction of the Persian belief in angels and intermediate spirits between God and men; or in the high place accorded to the Greek Wisdom. At the same time there were those who rebelled against this, and clung tenaciously to their old ideas.

Fourthly, there was deepening thought about the problem of suffering in the world, and about life after death. Both of these are well seen in the book of Job.

## PHARISAISM

The most important religious group of the time was the Pharisees—the word means 'separate', and they correspond in some ways to the later Puritans. The role they play in the New Testament has led some to underestimate them. They were a powerful and influential sect, with an exalted religion and a code of behaviour higher than most. They had a high belief in one god, whom they addressed as 'our father'. They insisted that religion had its outcome in morality, and that justice in the strict sense was not enough, but must be tempered by mercy. They believed in a future life, and they believed that few sins were beyond pardon.

At the same time they developed the institutions of religion. Alongside the temple at Jerusalem grew up local congregations or synagogues in which worship was carried on and instruction in the faith given. Further, they organized brotherhoods to stimulate worship and to practise social service. There were preaching tours, often by humble craftsmen, as with the Wesleyan Methodists centuries later. There was sick-visiting and prison-visiting, the reform of the penal code, an emphasis on education, and the establishment of the ancient equivalents of the Royal Society for the Prevention of Cruelty to Animals and the National Society for the Prevention of Cruelty to Children.

It was the work of the Pharisees which kept pure the core of Hebrew religion during the difficult centuries after the exile. It was their work, although it was in some ways negated by Jesus, which made possible the reforms of Jesus. It was their work which enabled the Jews to stand the shock of disastrous conflict with Rome and preserved the Jewish faith to this day.

## THE CONTRIBUTION OF THE JEWS

It is a grave mistake to suppose that all parts of the Old Testament are equally inspired. The Old Testament is the story of a pilgrimage, of a search for God, of a journey which starts from primitive tribal superstition and reaches a religion of great profundity and high morality.

If we want to sum up the vision which the Jews have given to the world we can hardly do it better than in an analysis by the great Old Testament scholar H. Wheeler Robinson. First, the vision of God, one God of all the world, Lord of nature, Lord of history and Lord of man, holy, righteous and loving. Second, the thought that man is utterly dependent on God, that he finds his fulfilment in accepting the moral imperative of God, and God's personal call to him. Third, the idea of the kingdom. God's purpose in history is a community of peace and social justice, in which God reigns, and which is ushered in by the perfect obedience of his Messiah. Finally, the growing realization of the place of redemptive suffering in human life; suffering is always a problem, especially when the innocent suffer, but the prophets came to see that it is possible by suffering oneself to help and even to save others.

# 3

# THE GREEKS

## GREEK GEOGRAPHY

GREEK history cannot be understood apart from Greek geography. Greece is a rough country with a number of comparatively small coastal plains shut off from one another by mountain-barriers which might be impassable in winter and difficult at any time. The smallness and isolation of these plains led the Greeks to think in terms of a limited political unit, which they called the *polis* (from which the word 'political' is derived), and which is conventionally translated 'city-state'. Aristotle, the greatest of Greek political theorists, said that a state of 100,000 citizens would no longer be a state, any more than a ship a quarter of a mile long would be a ship. We may laugh at such smallness of thought but we shall not understand the Greeks unless we learn to think in these terms.

This sense of a bounded world, combined with the sharp outlines created by the clear light of the Mediterranean, helped to create the peculiar quality of Greek thought. It is characteristic of the Greeks that to the major schools of philosophy limit or boundary is accounted good and its absence evil; the expansive outlook of modern times has tended to reverse this. A Greek temple is formally perfect; nothing can be added to it or taken from it without destroying its character. By contrast the Gothic cathedrals of western Europe grew across the centuries in a diversity of styles, and at Coventry and Cologne are still growing. Scenes can be cheerfully excised from Shakespeare's plays without destroying their sprawling genius; it would be impossible to 'cut' a Greek tragedy. Egyptian and Babylonian statues were intended to be seen in an architectural setting; the Greeks were the first people to make statues to be walked round and seen from all sides. Greek thinking is clear-cut and analytic, and this was the great contribution of the Greeks.

The temple of Hephaestus, god of fire, at Athens, known as the Theseum because its frieze depicted scenes from the life of Theseus. A fifth century B.C. Doric temple, it was built, like the Parthenon which it resembles, of white marble of astonishing brilliance and smoothness. For the Greeks the outside of a temple was far more important than the inside; they preferred a shrine of marvellous external beauty so placed as to dominate their daily lives rather than, as in Christian churches, a beautifully decorated interior calculated to encourage devotion and meditation.

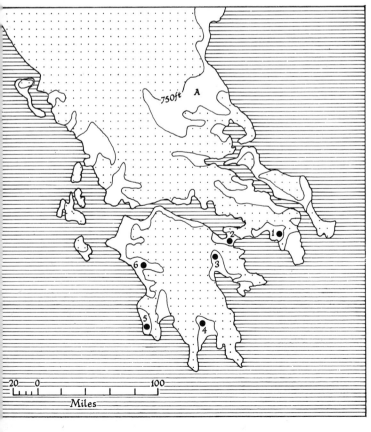

GREECE
1 Athens
2 Corinth
3 Mycenae
4 Sparta
5 Pylos
6 Olympia
A Plain of Thessaly

# ORIGINS

Sir John Myres wrote a book *Who were the Greeks?* It has been called the greatest detective-story ever written, with four possible solutions, all plausible and none proven. The most we can say for sure is that the Greeks were an Indo-European people who entered Greece in a series of waves from the middle of the second millennium B.C. They swept south until they came into contact with the power of Crete, borrowed the script they found there to write their own language, linked the earth-goddesses whom they found worshipped in different forms with their own sky-god Zeus, and made their main centres Mycenae in the east of Greece, and Pylos in the west; later, Sparta and Athens became more important.

## HOMER AND THE TROJAN WAR

The most famous episode of the early history of Greece was the war with Troy, whose traditional date lies in the twelfth century B.C. The occasion of the war may well have been the abduction of the Spartan queen Helen by a Trojan prince named Paris, but this was no more the real cause than the murder of an archduke in Sarajevo was the real cause of the First World War. Troy commanded the Dardanelles, and was in a position to make easy money by controlling the trade between the Black Sea and the Mediterranean; the war, bitter and long-lasting, freed the Greeks from the imposts of the Trojan middlemen.

Across the centuries ballad-mongers sang stories of the heroic age. About the ninth century a minstrel of genius named Homer put together a series of episodes from the Trojan War in his own way to make an artistic whole. At first sight the *Iliad* is just another bloodthirsty and exciting war-story, but at the last we realize that this is a war-story which is different. It is the story of how the brutal soldier Achilles learned to pity. The *Iliad* is the first great work of literary art from the western world. Most people today agree that it is essentially the work of one man, though he may have used earlier material, and there may have been later additions.

A rhapsode, minstrel, or ballad-singer, during a performance. The epic poetry of the Greeks began as improvised ballads sung by such minstrels in the camps and courts and on public occasions. The best ballads became traditional and widely known; by the time of Homer the minstrel's task was to reproduce traditional poetry from memory, linking the episodes with improvised passages of his own. Pictures of the earliest minstrels show them carrying a lyre, which suggests that their words were sung; later the lyre was replaced by a staff, as though the elaborate poetry of the later minstrels needed reciting, not singing. The ancient epic reached its climax in the mouth of Homer, a minstrel of genius; the *Iliad*, an epic of the Trojan war, and the *Odyssey* (which may be of different authorship), the story of the wanderings of the hero Odysseus, are among the finest literary achievements of man.

This fragment of an amphora is decorated in the Attic red-figure style of the fifth century B.C.

ACHILLES defeats and kills Penthesilea, queen of the Amazons. After the death of Hector the Amazons, a race of female warriors in Greek mythology who lived at the outer edge of the known world, came to the support of the Trojans and fought courageously until the death of their queen. Achilles, the ancient type of barbarous and brutal soldier, is represented by Lycophron as grieving for Penthesilea after her death.

Amazons were favourite subjects of Greek artists. This beautiful amphora (or two-handled pot) is decorated in the Attic black-figure style of the sixth century B.C. The figures were laid on in black paint and the detail picked out by incised lines.

PRIAM, king of Troy, kneels and begs Achilles to surrender, in exchange for lavish gifts, the body of his son Hector: a beautifully engraved cup showing this scene from the last book of the *Iliad*.

Hector's body has been dragged behind Achilles' racing chariot, and was intended for the dogs; and Priam, on learning of Hector's death, had befouled himself with dung: curious savageries (so they seem to us) to have been practised by a god-like hero and a noble monarch—and a hint of the strangeness of the Homeric world.

## COLONIZATION AND CIVILIZATION

The Greek farmers found themselves short of land, and their answer was to emigrate. All round the Mediterranean sprang up colonies, many destined to be famous in history. We may mention Massilia (the modern Marseilles), Naples (Nea-polis means 'the new city'; it was in fact a colony of a colony, being founded from nearby Cumae), Syracuse in Sicily, Byzantium (later Constantinople and today Istanbul) and Cyrene (the only colony in North Africa). This period of expansion is important not merely because it relieved the immediate economic situation, but because it gave the Greeks, through contact with other peoples, the needful stimulus to develop their civilization.

The first sign of something new is found on the coast of Asia Minor round about the year 600 B.C. Already there were signs of exciting developments in art. Decorated pottery was showing a new mastery of design. It was in western Asia that the Phoenicians had invented the alphabet. Now there was a growth of lyric poetry, whose supreme exponent was perhaps the greatest poetess of history, 'dark-haired, holy, sweetly smiling Sappho'.

> Like the sweet apple which reddens upon the topmost bough,
> A-top on the topmost twig—which the pluckers forgot somehow,—
> Forgot it not, nay, but got it not, for none could get it till now.
>
> Like the wild hyacinth flower, which on the hills is found,
> Which the passing feet of the shepherds for ever tear and wound,
> Until the purple blossom is trodden into the ground.

Not only so, but there emerged a group of men who began to ask quite new questions. Their leader was named Thales, from Miletus, and he began to ask 'What is the world made of and how does it change to become what it is?' This question is the spring of science and philosophy. It led men to observe nature, and across the next 200 years we have astonishingly detailed observations of fossils, and the percolation of water through rock, and the way caterpillars move, and the structure of an eagle's wings and much else. It also led men to think, and their thought, on purely logical grounds, brought them within two centuries to a theory of the atomic structure of the universe on which no substantial advance was made till about 1800.

## POLITICAL DEVELOPMENT

In general we can trace a well-marked pattern of political development in the Greek states. Usually there are signs of an early stage of monarchy. Then the barons rose to challenge the king, somewhat as happened in England at the time of Magna Carta. The office of king was either eliminated or reduced to religious functions or (occasionally) left with shorn powers. Economic misery led to restlessness among the poorer classes. Not yet politically organized, they supported a leader who voiced their discontent and established himself as dictator, or, in the Greek word, 'tyrant'. Good dictators were followed by bad dictators and revolution by counter-revolution. But the people were on the march, and the classical period of the fifth century B.C. saw the Greek states swaying between the oligarchs (oligarchy means 'the rule of a small number'), who wished power to be confined to a relatively small class, and the democrats (democracy means 'the authority of the commons') who stood for a wider and more radical extension of power.

The words 'extension of power' are used advisedly. Citizen-rights were jealously guarded in democracies as in oligarchies, and a democracy was only an extended oligarchy. Women had no part in politics. Aliens were seldom allowed the rights of citizens, and underlying the whole structure of society was a foundation of slavery. All these lacked political rights, but were not necessarily oppressed in other ways. Slaves formed the civil service, and, at Athens, even the police, and much business was carried on by aliens.

## SPARTA

In the sixth and early fifth centuries the dominant power in Greece was Sparta, a city of the south. Sparta did not go through the normal process of development; she was what Arnold Toynbee has called an 'arrested civilization'. In the economic crises of the eighth century B.C. Sparta chose to conquer her land-neighbours rather than expand overseas. The danger of revolt from her subjects changed the whole course of Spartan history. Sparta became a state organized with unusual thoroughness for military power.

The political constitution scarcely matters. There were kings, two of them, with enormous prestige but limited powers. There was an assembly of the whole citizen-body, an apparently democratic touch, but its powers were small. There was a senate comprising the two kings and twenty-eight elders, in whom the power of government was vested. The real authority lay with five ephors or superintendents. They controlled finance, education, the police and foreign policy, and had the right to depose the kings for unconstitutional action.

The total number of citizens can never have been above 10,000 at the utmost. In the fifth century it was more like 5000; by the mid-fourth century it declined to under 1000. (By contrast it is reasonable to suppose about 43,000 citizens in Athens in 431 B.C.). Culture and education were directed to military prowess, though music was developed as a relaxation; there was training in discipline and physical toughness. Communal messes fostered national unity. Women were given more freedom than in most of the Greek world. They too were trained to toughness. A Spartan girl appears in an Athenian comedy:

> Lampito, my sweet! Delighted to see you, darling,
> How pretty you look! How healthy you Spartans are!
> And my, what biceps! I believe you could throttle a bull.

The freedom of women meant that love-marriages were possible in Sparta, whereas in the rest of the Greek world marriage was often a family arrangement. This was some compensation for a system which seems to us distasteful. Yet the Spartans won the admiration of many ancient philosophers, perhaps because their state was organized purposively to a deliberate end. They have left little directly to posterity, much indirectly.

Typical of the things for which Sparta stood is the story of Leonidas. With 6000 men he held the narrow pass of Thermopylae against a Persian army overwhelmingly larger, till a traitor led the Persians by a mountain-track so as to surround them. There was now no hope, but they fought to the death rather than surrender. One of the Spartans, being told that the Persians were so numerous that their arrows blotted out the light of the sun, said that it would be pleasanter in the shade. Over these Spartans the epitaph was written:

> Stranger, in Lacedaemon be it heard
> We lie here, bowing to their every word.

Such was Spartan courage and Spartan discipline.


## THE CHALLENGE FROM THE OUTSIDE

The Greeks, however much they might differ among themselves, were proudly nationalistic as a whole. The Greek language is a remarkable instrument for elegant, delicate and precise expression, and the Greeks considered those to whom it was not native as babblers, *barbaroi*, barbarians, the people who utter unintelligible noises such as 'bar-bar-bar'. By contrast 'Hellenic' (the Greek name for themselves was 'Hellenes') became equivalent to 'cultured'.

Other forces made for the unity of Greece. The Olympic Games, which are still celebrated today, started in 776 B.C. People came, once every four years, from all over the Greek world to compete, and during the competitions a universal truce was proclaimed. The famous oracle at Delphi was honoured by all the Greeks, and came to be associated with an attitude to life summarized in the phrases 'Know yourself' and 'Avoid excess'. The priests had their contacts all over the Greek world and were able to give sensible advice; when in doubt, they sometimes spoke ambiguously. King Croesus of Lydia was told that by declaring war he would destroy a mighty kingdom. He did—his own.

In the early fifth century the Greeks of the mainland were threatened by Persia. Facing great odds, through the skill of the Athenian sailors and the disciplined courage of the Spartan soldiers, they won, and the preliminary skirmish at Marathon in 490 B.C., and the main engagements at Salamis in 480 and Plataea in 479 are written among the decisive battles of the world. Dr Johnson wrote: 'The man is little to be envied whose patriotism would not gain force upon the plain at Marathon.' Meantime in Sicily the Greek settlers were simultaneously repelling the power of Carthage, a colony of the Phoenicians in North Africa. These military victories were victories for liberty, however uncomfortable, over autocracy, however benevolent; they made possible both the flowering of culture at Athens and the wars and conflicts which followed the abuse of freedom.

## ATHENIAN DEMOCRACY

Athens passed through the typical phases of Greek development. About 594 B.C. a middle-of-the-road politician named Solon unsuccessfully attempted a patchwork solution of economic and political difficulties. He failed, but the dictatorship of Pisistratus (d. 527 B.C.) made for political progress and attracted men of culture from all over the Greek world to Athens. The middle of the fifth century saw in Athens a democracy perhaps more radical than the world has ever known. All power lay in the assembly, where all adult male citizens had the right to speak (though it seems that not many used this right) and to vote. In addition these same citizens formed the juries in the law-courts, where recalcitrant politicians might find themselves on trial. Payment

The Athenian Acropolis showing, in the centre, the ruined Parthenon, temple of Athena (*parthenos* = a virgin), the most celebrated of all the great Greek temples. An acropolis was originally a fortified hill near a city's precincts where civilians could shelter in the event of an attack. The acropolis at Athens, which lies just to the south of the city, was from very early times part citadel and part sanctuary. In the great flowering of Athenian civilization under Pericles a plan for new building was put in hand which, for the beauty and magnificence of the architecture, made the Athenian Acropolis one of the glories of the ancient world. The approach to the Parthenon was through the Propylaea—a great roofed colonnade visible on the left. On a bastion in front of this can be seen the tiny temple of Victory, and in the background, between the Propylaea and the Parthenon, the Erechtheum, dedicated to Erechtheus, a legendary king of Athens.

was made for attendance, a truly democratic move making the right of the poor to attend practical as well as theoretical. All offices were filled by lot from the whole citizen-body; each citizen had an equal chance of finding himself on the governing council, and indeed, for one day, presiding over it; the only exceptions were a few insignificant priesthoods, and the military commanders, who were elected annually. In addition, a curious device known as ostracism protected the country from dictatorship; a dangerous or unpopular figure might be blackballed by popular vote and deported for ten years without losing his rights on his eventual return. An amusing story recorded how a peasant voted against a politician of unusual integrity, because he was 'so fed up with hearing him called the Incorruptible'; another how a less scrupulous politician organized an ostracism to get rid of one of his two political opponents, and was himself ostracized when they formed a coalition against him.

Such a political system may be criticized in many ways. It was notoriously unstable; once, in 427 B.C., an order for the mass execution of rebellious subjects was passed one day and revoked the next—just in time. But it can hardly be denied that it was democratic, and one wonders by what right any modern state calls itself by that name. 'America', said T. R. Glover, 'lacks the two essential qualities of a democracy; the people there neither make the laws nor interpret them', and the same applies to Britain, the Soviet Union and India. Athens did enjoy government of the people, by the people, for the people.

PERICLES of Athens (about 490–429 B.C.). The leadership of Athens in the Greek world was the guiding principle of Pericles's life. He founded important colonies. He initiated vast building projects, including the Parthenon and the Propylaea, and made Athens the most beautiful and impressive city in the world. When the Peloponnesian War broke out he devised and controlled the whole Athenian strategy until the city's morale broke in the disastrous plague of 430. Driven from office, he was recalled a few months later; but by then he was suffering from the plague himself, and he died in the summer of 429.

His greatness must be measured in the highest terms. He was incorruptible. His mind was penetrating and incisive. He was a remarkable orator and a man of wide culture. The judgment of Thucydides—'Athens was ruled by her greatest citizen'—still stands.

Stability was given by outstanding leadership freely accepted. Pericles (d. 429 B.C.) was the great statesman of the day and his ideal for his country has passed into the imperishable statements of the human spirit:

Our constitution is named a democracy, because it is in the hands not of the few but of the many. But our laws secure equal justice for all in their private disputes, and our public opinion welcomes and honours talent in every branch of achievement, not for any sectional reason, but on grounds of excellence alone. And as we give free play to all in our public life, so we carry the same spirit into our daily relations with one another.... Open and friendly in our private intercourse, in our public acts we keep strictly within the control of law.... Yet ours is no work-a-day city only. No other provides so many recreations for the spirit—contests and sacrifices all the year round, and beauty in our public buildings to cheer the heart and delight the eye day by day....We are lovers of beauty without extravagance, and lovers of wisdom without unmanliness....In a word I claim that our city as a whole is an education to Greece, and that her members yield to none, man by man, for independence of spirit, many-sidedness of attainment, and complete self-reliance in limbs and brain.

## ATHENIAN CULTURE

The 120 years from 470 to 350 B.C. saw in Athens a flowering of artistic talent never surpassed, and never equalled in a community of comparable size. All were Greek; most, though not all, were Athenian born. In tragic drama there are only three figures from the whole of the rest of the world at any time we can put alongside Aeschylus, Sophocles and Euripides; in comic drama scarcely any alongside Aristophanes; Herodotus (a foreigner) and Thucydides created the science of history; Pericles and Demosthenes rank with Cicero, Burke and Churchill as political orators; Socrates, Plato and Aristotle (another foreigner) have had more influence on human thought than any other group of three philosophers; of the architect Ictinus we know little, but the Parthenon is his enduring monument; in sculpture Phidias and Praxiteles may be mentioned in the same breath as Donatello, Michelangelo and Rodin, and not many others.

The achievement is staggering. It has never been properly explained. No doubt the peculiar characteristics of Greek geography made their contribution; but there has been nothing comparable out of Greece since. No doubt

41

the quality of Greek democracy threw up outstanding individuals: this was seen as an explanation in the ancient world itself. No doubt the mood of the times played its part; there is something comparable in England at the end of the sixteenth century. But something is left unexplained. One thing can be said: Athenian culture is infectious—the Italian Renaissance and the rebirth of drama in modern France are but two examples of a flame lit by contact with the Greeks. A great monarch called Athens 'the beacon-tower of the world'.

## DRAMA

No one knows for certain the origins of Greek drama. It is clear only that they were religious; they may have been connected with some fertility ritual. Religious dance-dramas, often re-enacting some myth, are found in Africa today. The earliest plays seem concerned with the fate of the chorus. This may indicate that drama arose from choral song; first the chorus-leader and then other actors became detached from the singers. As drama developed interest shifted to the actors and the chorus provided a commentary upon the action or, perhaps, little more than an interlude in the action.

Greek drama was highly stylized. Theatres were built of stone, in the open air, often in a natural semicircle in the hillside; acoustics were superb. Actors were severely limited in number, but might double parts; the masks they wore made this easier. Facial expression was not used, gestures were broad and sweeping, much depended on vocal rhetoric. Aeschylus was noted for his magniloquent language, Euripides for his skill in debate. At the dramatic festivals each playwright submitted a group of three plays or trilogy, with a humorous satyr-play appended.

The three great Athenian tragedians were in strong contrast to one another. Aeschylus was a philosopher, Sophocles a dramatist, and Euripides a propagandist, but each was a superb master of theatrical technique. It happens that we have a surviving play about Electra from each of the three, which points the contrast. Agamemnon, commander of the Greeks at Troy, has been murdered by his wife Clytemnestra and her lover Aegisthus. By the standards of early society Agamemnon's children, Orestes and Electra, have

DELPHI: the theatre in the foreground, and, behind, the pillars of the Temple of Apollo.

A performance of a classical Greek tragedy in the theatre of Epidaurus. The restored theatre seats 15,000 people, and has perfect acoustics. It is 360 feet across.

a duty to avenge him. But to do so, they must kill their own mother. To Aeschylus the theme presents a moral problem which he poses with terrifying power. Sophocles pushes the death of the mother into the background, and concentrates upon the dramatic irony to be drawn from the death of Aegisthus. To Euripides the murder of Clytemnestra is a crime and he blazons it as such, and draws out the psychology of children who would commit such an act. Thus we have three plays on the same theme, markedly different from one another, but very powerful.

The older comedies were racy and uproarious, with a serious social purpose underlying them. Aristophanes' most famous plays deal with new fashions in education (*The Clouds*), the longing for escape from contemporary society (*The Birds*), the emancipation of women (*Lysistrata*), and literary standards (*The Frogs*). Later, political comment declined and with it the motive force of the most brilliant comedy.

44

# ART AND ARCHITECTURE

Greek architecture, judged from its public buildings, has three main styles: the Doric, simple, solid and enduring; the Ionic, light and graceful; and the elaborate Corinthian. The contrast may be seen in the capitals which topped the columns. The Doric has plain cushion capitals, the Ionic twirling rams' horns at the corner, the Corinthian a complex pattern of acanthus leaves. All three styles are to be seen in Athens. The Parthenon is Doric; the Erechtheum and the exquisite little temple of Wingless Victory are Ionic; the colossal remains of the temple of Olympian Zeus are Corinthian. The temples, apparently simple, conceal a mastery of optical illusion. The base, which appears straight, is convex, the columns lean inwards and bulge in the centre, the corner-columns are thicker than the others. Yet the whole effect is one of perfect harmony.

Some of the finest Greek sculpture was associated with these temples, either in the form of temple-images like Phidias's famous Athena Parthenos or in the pediments (triangular spaces over the front and back which presented an

Goddesses from the Parthenon sculptures, once called *The Three Fates*. The figures are meant to fit into the acute angle at the base of the pediment. Note how the sculptor has made this 'fit'. Note too the beauty of the drapery.

45

interesting challenge to the designer) or in a frieze running round the building. The finest surviving frieze comes from the Parthenon and shows the Panathenaic procession; some of it was rescued from destruction by Lord Elgin, and is to be seen in the British Museum. We may particularly admire the superb skill with which the horsemen are represented, as we may admire the brilliant design and execution of a group of three goddesses (formerly called the Three Fates) which fitted a corner of one pediment.

# HUMANISM

The fifth and fourth centuries saw an increasing interest in man as well as the material world. We can see it in sculpture; the old stylized portrayals of the gods give way to their picture as a type of ideal humanity, and then in the fourth century as humanity unadorned. We can see it in the rise of itinerant lecturers, called 'sophists', who claimed to prepare men for life and, being sceptical about religion, trained them in values which were purely human. We can see it above all in Socrates. Cicero said of him that he brought philosophy down from heaven and planted it upon the earth; that is, he was concerned with man and not physical astronomy.

Socrates (469–399 B.C.) was the son of a stone-mason and a midwife. He said of himself that he was an intellectual midwife; he claimed to teach nothing himself and left no writings, but he helped others to give birth to the ideas which were inside them. At first interested in science, he found himself asking 'Why?' as well as 'How?' and science cannot answer that question. He was puzzled, at a loss. Then a friend asked the Delphic oracle whether there was anyone wiser than Socrates; the oracle said 'No'. Socrates, unable to find the answers himself, started asking questions, and found that others could not give the answers either. He would ask a soldier 'What is courage?' or a religious leader 'What is piety?' and find that they did not really know, for all their pomp and bluster. So he concluded that he really was the wisest man in Greece; no one knew anything, but he at least knew that he knew nothing. Two things stand out about him: his care for men and the well-being of their soul or personality, and his confidence in reason. They executed him because he could not stand the slipshod practices of democratic Athens; his

46

Socrates, to us the most familiar figure of the Greek world, has survived entirely in the writings of others, notably Plato and Xenophon. Although the significance of Socrates' thought is difficult to determine, his influence on the thought of his successors has undoubtedly been very great. As a man he was physically and morally strong, courageous, kindly, with a sense of duty and outstanding intellectual ability; as a philosopher he was both moralist and logician, devoting his great gifts to formulating the basis of morality and the nature of knowledge. Love of truth was the key to his life.

criticisms had been absorbed by men less scrupulous than he, who had done the state much harm. He went cheerfully to his death, spending his last hours in discussing the immortality of the soul.

Aristotle said of Socrates that his importance in the history of thought lay in his power to see patterns, to pick out the general principle underlying a set of events or similar objects (all scientific theory consists in this). What is a horse? What is it that makes all horses similar to one another and different from donkeys? What makes all just actions similar to one another and different from unjust actions? This was indeed important. But Socrates' real importance lies not in what he *said* or *did* but in what he *was*. Those closest to him join in saying 'He was the best man I ever knew'. He had strong feelings and stronger self-control. He was at once a rationalist and a mystic. He was courageous, quizzical and absolutely honest. The impress of his personality remains with us today.


## THE SYSTEM-MAKERS

The most remarkable of Socrates' associates was Plato (427–347 B.C.). To him it was given to create a mighty system of thought. According to Plato the material world in which we live is an imperfect reflection of the perfect world of 'forms'. We are (to adapt his example) like people who live their lives in a cinema looking at celluloid figures reflected on a screen. Reality is outside, in the sunlight.

> What if Earth
> Be but the shaddow of Heav'n, and things therein
> Each to other like, more than on Earth is thought?

Horses are like one another because they 'imitate' or 'share in' the perfect Horse, the 'form' of Horse. Just actions are like one another because they 'imitate' or 'share in' the 'form' of Justice. With our senses we perceive the physical world; we must discipline our intelligences to perceive the real world of perfection, and Plato told a critic who claimed to know the things of the material world but not the 'forms', that this was because he had eyes but no intelligence. The man who so disciplines himself 'will see a Beauty eternal, not growing or decaying, waxing or waning....Beauty absolute, separate, simple and everlasting; which lending of its virtue to all beautiful things which we see born to decay, itself suffers neither increase nor diminution, nor any other change.' 'There the soul beholds true justice, true moderation and knowledge—not the sort of knowledge that is always changing and is attached to the various things we commonly call real, but knowledge in the fullest sense of that which exists in the fullest sense.'

Plato founded a residential university, the Academy. His outstanding pupil was a doctor's son from the far north, Aristotle (384–322 B.C.). Aristotle was a great scientist; Charles Darwin compared him with a schoolmaster to whom all that followed were but schoolboys. His account of cuttle-fish is a classic piece of zoological observation, minute and precise, and including details which remained unconfirmed for more than two thousand years. Like any good scientist, Aristotle started from facts; he is as interested in the world of things as Plato in the world of ideas, and his political theory and his literary criticism, for instance, are based on a wide acquaintance with current practice. He too built a system. He saw the universe as a great chain of being, from pure formless matter at the bottom, to God at the top, who moves the universe, himself unmoved, as a girl may move the emotions of a boy while remaining herself indifferent. In ethics he defined virtue as a state or habit of action, arising from deliberate choice, and lying in a mean between two extremes. The man who is brave is neither rash nor cowardly; he has chosen in the past to be a brave man, but he does not have to choose afresh each time—his virtue is a state or habit. This is sound commonsense morality.

Plato and Aristotle were living in an age of change. Each believed passionately in the city-state. They tried to find ways of pegging back the march of history, of preventing the city-state from vanishing. We can see this in their political writings (Plato thought that the only hope was for philosophers to become kings, or kings philosophers); we can see too that the unchanging forms and the unmoved mover were the aspirations of men whose world was changing, moving, crumbling. Their world disappeared; yet their discussions of politics, as of much else, are still relevant and their vision has remained to inspire others.

## THE END OF THE CITY-STATE

The last part of the fifth century saw a long and bitter war between Sparta and Corinth on the one hand (Corinth was an economic rival of Athens) and Athens and the naval empire she had acquired on the other. The war brought a breakdown of moral values, as war always does. Both sides were weakened. Persia re-emerged in Greek affairs. Plato lived his life amid scenes of shifting power and growing uncertainty. The great educationalist Isocrates (436–338 B.C.) pleaded for the unity of Greece; he was a voice crying in the wilderness. At Athens the brilliant orator and unscrupulous opportunist Demosthenes (383–322 B.C.) ousted wiser statesmen, and eventually Greece had unity imposed on her by the military power of Macedon in the north, just as in nineteenth-century Africa tribal jealousies laid the way open for the colonial imperialists. The day of the city-state was done; the era of world-thinking was dawning.


## THE GREEK ACHIEVEMENT

The Greek achievement may be summed up under two heads. In the first place the Greeks made beautiful things, without pursuing idle theories of abstract beauty. 'The Greek temple', writes Nikolaus Pevsner, 'is the most perfect example ever achieved of architecture finding its fulfilment in bodily beauty', and Sir John Beazley remarked of a Greek vase that it was not possible to draw better, only differently. The point need not be laboured; it is there, in architecture, in sculpture, in painting, in poetry.

Second and more important, the great Greeks were rationalists. Of course we can find traces of irrationalism in Greek society. But many people have been irrational; few have been as systematically rational as the Greeks, and here, not in the other, their distinctive achievement lies. They asked questions, curious questions like Thales, awkward questions like Socrates. 'After all', said one of them, 'isn't a question a sort of education?' As C. F. Angus used to say, the Greeks had that divine unfaith which has also moved mountains.

They were not content with inadequate answers. Epilepsy was called the 'sacred disease'; it was thought to be a direct visitation from some god. A Greek doctor writes, 'It seems to me that the disease is no more divine than any other. It has a natural cause, just as other diseases have. Men think it divine merely because they do not understand it. But if they called everything divine which they do not understand—why, there would be no end of divine things.'

In this restless questioning spirit, and the belief that reason can find the answer, lies the real importance of the Greeks. For curiosity is the beginning of philosophy, and reason the foundation of science. 'To one small people it was given to create the forces of progress: that people was the Greek.'

THE HERMES OF PRAXITELES. This is the only original work of a Greek master-sculptor of the classical period preserved to us. Other works are known to us only in reproductions made in the Hellenistic and Roman periods. This was not one of the artist's greatest works, and its quality shows how wonderful those must have been.

# 4

# THE HELLENISTIC AGE

## ALEXANDER

THE accidents of history have given the nickname 'the Great' to some curious people, to Pompey but not to Caesar, to Constantine but not to Augustus, to Basil but not to Augustine. Few have deserved it as thoroughly as Alexander (356–323 B.C.), king of Macedon. He was only twenty-one when he turned the armies of Greece eastward; he was only thirty-two when he died. At the beginning of those eleven years Greek thinking was parochial; at the end of them it was global.

Considered merely as an epic of travel his story is breath-taking. He swept criss-cross up and down in a great cock-eyed M movement through Asia Minor, down Palestine into Egypt and far into the Libyan desert to Siwa. Then he swung back round the Fertile Crescent through Mesopotamia

The routes of Alexander and his army.

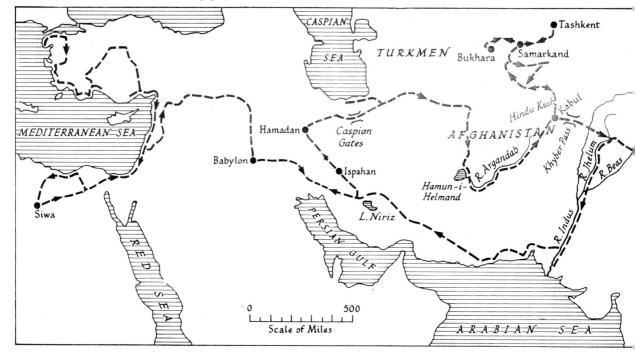

ALEXANDER. From the bust in the museum at Istanbul. Alexander was only 32 when he died. The sculptor was obviously deeply impressed by this quality of youthful achievement.

to the edge of the Persian Gulf; then across to Lake Niriz, back through Ispahan and Hamadan, east through the Caspian Gates to the south-east corner of the Caspian Sea, east again into Turkmenistan, hundreds of miles south through Afghanistan to Hanum-i-Helmand, turning north-east up the valley of the Argandab. Next, in a series of incredible marches he pushed through the Hindu Kush and passed Bukhara and Samarkand, and all but reached Tashkent. Here he retraced his steps, but at Kabul pushed east through the Khyber into India, across the Indus, across the Jhelum to the Beas. At this point his troops had had enough; even Alexander's magnetism could not hold them; he was forced to turn back. But they were not done yet; it was down the Jhelum and the Indus to the coast, and then in a march of terrible suffering back to Lake Niriz and Babylon, where he died. He had covered 12,000 miles in ten years, with an army, fighting all the way, founding cities as he went.

# ALEXANDER'S ACHIEVEMENT

As a military commander Alexander stands among the supreme few. He broke the military might of Persia against large odds in three encounters. His speed of movement was astonishing—400 miles in eleven days pursuing the Persians, 180 miles in three days to relieve Samarkand. He showed great versatility: twice he took by siege fortresses which were thought impregnable. His own courage was the example to his men; unlike the Duke of Plaza-Toro, he led his regiment from in front.

Yet, if this were all, Alexander would not merit our interest. He had a constructive vision as well as a destructive genius. This developed during his life. In his youth he had been a pupil of Aristotle, who taught him that the 'barbarian', the non-Greek, was designed by nature to be a slave. He crossed the Dardanelles, with Homer under his pillow, with the simple aim of conquering Persia in the name of Greek civilization. As he advanced he met opponents whom he could respect and administrators whom he could trust—and he found that some of his Greeks had feet of clay. So he came to trust Persians with administration, to admit them into his army, to encourage (and practise) mixed marriage. But this policy of fusion was, or became, part of a wider vision. He no longer said that the Greek was the only real man, and the 'barbarian' scarcely man at all, but that the good man was the only true Greek, and the bad man the only true barbarian. He believed that he had a mission from God to bring general harmony and to be 'the reconciler of the world'. In that remarkable phrase is summed up Alexander's belief in the brotherhood of man under the fatherhood of God.

As Alexander lay ill they asked an oracle if he should be moved. The reply was 'No, for that is best'. Two days later he died, for that was best. 'Whom the gods love, die young.' What he would have achieved had he lived is unimaginable. As it was, he left the world a different place.

# THE HELLENISTIC AGE

Alexander's empire broke into warring kingdoms. The fringes fell away, though the impress of the Greek was left upon the art of India. The age which followed is called the Hellenistic Age. It was marked among the Greeks by what has been termed 'the failure of nerve'. The old values, the old certainties, were gone. It was not that there was nothing to take their place, rather that there was too much. The *polis*, the city-state, was broken, swamped by the great kingdoms which followed Alexander's empire. Men felt themselves in the grip of power-politics which they could not control. Faith in the old gods, associated with the life of the city, was broken. New gods swept in from all the world over, with a multitude of *daemons* (hence the word 'demon') or intermediate spirits. Chance—Luck—was worshipped as a divinity. Men feared life; the thoughtful defied it like the Cynics, grimly accepted it like the Stoics, or retreated from it like the Epicureans. All were seeking *autarky*, self-sufficiency, independence, what Aldous Huxley calls 'non-attachment'. It is an age of uncertainty, of questing; which helps to explain Christianity's triumph when it brought answers of certainty.

THE SCHOOL OF ATHENS, by Raphael: one of the artist's enormous dramatic groups. In a grandiose architectural setting—a great perspective of arches through which the open sky appears—all the great Athenian philosophers are imagined, disputing, teaching, meditating.

In the very centre are Plato and Aristotle. Plato points to the heavens, the home of absolute truth and ideal form. Aristotle's right arm is extended, palm down, to indicate that all experience is gained on this earth. Diogenes lies in rags on the steps. To the left above, Socrates, bald, snubnosed and bearded, as in the statuette reproduced on p. 47 above, instructs his followers. In the left foreground Pythagoras stands dominating a group of seated followers. On the right are the geometers and astronomers.

# THE CYNICS

In some ways the most characteristic sect of the age was the Cynic. The word, which has changed its meaning today, denotes something like 'dogged'. The founder of the sect, Diogenes (*c.* 395–320 B.C.) was nicknamed Diogenes the Dog because of his unconventional behaviour; he accepted the name: 'I lick the hands of the generous, bark at the stingy, and bite scoundrels.' His father, a finance-officer, had had to put counterfeit coin out of circulation. Diogenes set himself to do the same in the field of morals. So he flouted conventions and set himself to live naturally, and, in a world in which possessions were insecure, subsisted without possessions except for scrip and staff, and the famous jar in which he sheltered. He refused political rights and political responsibilities, calling himself 'a citizen of the universe'. He was 'as free as a bird, unconstrained by law, undisturbed by politicians'. Discipline and hardship made him tough, ready for anything that life could do to him.

> Therefore, since the world has still
> Much good, but much less good than ill,
> And while the sun and moon endure
> Luck's a chance, but trouble's sure,
> I'd face it as a wise man would,
> And train for ill and not for good.

Those words of A. E. Housman mirror the mood of the Hellenistic Age. Those who claimed to follow Diogenes included men who shocked for the sake of shocking, men who begged because it paid, men in whose lives simplicity degenerated into squalor. But they also included men of high moral fervour, who preached a way of salvation and practised what they preached.

# THE STOICS

More important were the Stoics, followers of Zeno (*c.* 300 B.C.), a man who, as was said at his funeral, 'had made his life an example to all, for he followed his own teaching'.

The Stoics were pantheists. Alexander Pope summed up the philosophy well in the words

> All are but part of one stupendous whole
> Whose body Nature is, and God the soul.

But if all is of God, then all is for the best, and indeed cannot be different.

> All nature is but art, unknown to thee,
> All chance, direction which thou canst not see;
> All discord, harmony not understood;
> All partial evil, universal good:
> And spite of pride, in erring reason's spite,
> One truth is clear—whatever is, is right.

In such a world, man's duty is to submit. The Stoic, like Thomas Carlyle's acquaintance, cried 'I accept the universe'. ('By God, she'd better,' said Carlyle.) Man must live according to nature, according to reason, according to God—the words mean the same. The external events of his life are determined; willy-nilly, he is a counter in the divine game of draughts. Hence the Stoic hymn:

> Lead me, O Zeus, and thou, O Destiny,
> > Lead thou me on.
> To whatsoever task thou sendest me
> > Lead thou me on.
> I follow fearless, or, if in mistrust
> I lag and will not, follow still I must.

One thing God cannot or will not determine—our acceptance. He will have our obedience; he wants our free obedience. 'This view', wrote Gilbert Murray, 'is so sublime and so stirring that at times it almost deadens one's powers of criticism.'

The Stoic answer to the quest then was: 'All is for the best, though it may not seem so. Accept, and give thanks to God.' Stoicism is in many ways an exalted philosophy: the Stoics took up Alexander's vision of the brotherhood of man, and claimed that at the last nothing mattered except virtue. But their teaching about acceptance prevented them from being reformers, and though, for instance, they held in theory that the slave was brother to the slave-owner, in practice they did nothing to abolish slavery.


## THE EPICUREANS

In contrast with Zeno stands his contemporary Epicurus (341–270 B.C.). Man's life, said Epicurus, is disturbed. What disturbs it? Two things: fear—

fear of the gods, fear of death and fear of pain—and desire outrunning its natural bounds. How can we overcome these? We can overcome fear by knowledge: if we have a properly scientific understanding of the world we shall know that the thunderstorms and eclipses in which superstitious people see the anger of the gods have natural explanations, that death is the end of life and no more to be feared than a dreamless sleep, and that pain at least cannot be both intense and long-lasting ('if it is sharp it is short; if it is long it is light'). We can overcome desire by realizing that most desires are unnecessary; we can free ourselves from ambition by living in retirement; we can be rid of crude desire by living the simple life.

It is commonly said of the Epicureans that they were atheists and pleasure-seekers. Both statements are lies and libels. Epicurus believed that superstition had done much harm in the world. But he believed in gods, too exalted to be interested in man, but remaining in the background as an influence for good and a standard of all that is best. Epicurus did indeed sometimes speak as if the aim of life were pleasure. But this was never crudely conceived. He himself said: 'It is impossible to live a happy life without living wisely, well, justly.' The man who lived on plain bread, because he then got so much pleasure from a gift of cheese, was no crude pleasure-seeker. The one pleasure he allowed complete freedom was friendship. 'Friendship goes dancing round the world, proclaiming to us all to awake to the praises of the happy life.' The Epicureans in many ways resembled the Quakers: they were a Society of Friends. They are on the whole the most attractive of ancient thinkers, but it is difficult not to feel that they were in some ways running away from life.


## POLITICAL DEVELOPMENT IN GREECE

The Greek states had lost their independence, but there was still room for experiment, especially when the imperial power was busy elsewhere. The two most significant experiments belong to the third century B.C., and are associated with two remarkable men, Aratus of Sicyon and Cleomenes III of Sparta.

Aratus stood for freedom and federalism, freedom from imperialism and federated equality between the newly freed states. He raised revolt in the cities of south Greece, and linked the liberated lands in a federal league. The central government was responsible for foreign policy, but the member states governed their own internal affairs. Here was a method which might combine the old values of the city-state and its intense local loyalty with the new values of Alexander's world in which the barriers were down.

Cleomenes stood for social justice. He carried out a communistic revolution in conservative Sparta. He broke the power of the governing clique, cancelled debts (nearly always owed by poor farmers to capitalist money-lenders), and redivided the land, abolishing the influence of the great land-owners and giving to every citizen a piece of land which he could call his own.

Tragically, the two movements came into conflict with one another. They need not have done so, but Cleomenes was ambitious for Spartan nationalism and Aratus sought personal power for himself. They clashed, and in the clash Macedon returned to power and undid the work of both.

## HELLENISTIC LITERATURE AND ART

An age is revealed in its art, and we may learn something of the Hellenistic Age from its literature and sculpture, which, without reaching the standards of classical Greece, had qualities of their own. From the literature of the period we may single out three features. First, a certain concise elegance, which meant that the outstanding literary achievement of later Greek writing lay in the epigram. We may see this in the golden phrases coined by the dramatist Menander (c. 342–292 B.C.); Paul quotes one, 'Evil communications corrupt good manners' or rather 'Bad company corrupts good character'. It is the mark of the shorter poems of Callimachus (c. 310–240 B.C.), the typical poet of the age. Second, we find a parade of curious learning (such as is found in other ages: John Donne and T. S. Eliot furnish examples); this is the sign of an age which is still asking questions, but, being uncertain of itself, wishes to show that it has found some answers. Third, there is a preoccupation with the human. A later critic said of Menander's plays: 'Menander! Life! I wonder which of you copied which.' The novel began to emerge as an art form. Poems and sketches were written about two gossiping women out sightseeing, or a schoolboy receiving a whacking, or a fisherman in his hut, and the only important epic of the period, the *Argonautica* of Apollonius, shows a conscious attempt to understand the psychology of the heroine.

LAOCOÖN, a prince of Troy, and his two sons, are destroyed by giant snakes: an episode recorded in the second book of Vergil's *Aeneid*. According to Vergil, Laocoön was punished for advising against drawing the wooden horse into the city. The original of this famous statue, which depicts the prince and his sons in their death agony, was the work of three Rhodian sculptors at the end of the first century.

The winged Nike, or Victory, of Samothrace, one of the great works of the Hellenistic Age.

The sculpture shows a restless searching for new themes; classical restraint has gone. We may think of the tortured agony of Laocoön and his sons in the grip of snakes; the portrayal of children, one struggling with a goose, another pulling a thorn from his foot; the massive boxers; the studies of simple workers, an old shepherdess, and a fisherman; the rendering of drunkenness, suicide, ecstasy, sleep. That beauty was not forgotten is seen in two world-famous statues, now in the Louvre in Paris, the Winged Victory in which 'Triumph is glorified, as never before or since' and the Venus de Milo.


## HELLENISTIC SCIENCE

Hellenistic art and literature fell away a little from what had gone before. But during this period Greek science reached its highest point.

In mathematics Euclid (*c.* 300 B.C.) put together the work of earlier scholars with such rigid logic that his book could still be used as a textbook of geometry even in the twentieth century.

In physical science Archimedes (*c.* 287–212 B.C.) ranks as the outstanding scholar of ancient times. His most famous achievements were three. He invented a spiral pump for raising water from the Nile; such a pump is still called 'Archimedes' screw'. He knew that he could move a great weight by a small force applied at a distance (he moved a large ship by a system of pulleys) and so boasted: 'Give me somewhere to stand and I will move the earth.' He was challenged to find out whether a crown was made of pure gold; sitting in his bath, he noticed the water rise and spill over, and realized that if the crown were not pure gold it would occupy more volume than an equal weight of pure gold (in scientific terms, it would have a smaller specific gravity) and would thus displace more water; according to story he jumped out of the bath and ran home without any clothes on, shouting '*Heureka!* *Heureka!*' 'I've got it! I've got it!'

In astronomy Aristarchus (*c.* 310–230 B.C.) came to the view that the sun remains fixed in position and the earth circles round it, an astonishing piece of insight. Rather later, Hipparchus (second century B.C.), perhaps the greatest astronomer of antiquity, made and recorded a wonderful series of detailed observations of the stars.

# ALEXANDRIA

The typical city of the Hellenistic Age is not Athens or Sparta, but Alexander's most famous foundation, Alexandria in Egypt. One enthusiast claims that Alexandria *is* the world: the whole earth is her territory, the other cities her suburbs.

Alexandria was a planned city—the Hellenistic Age loved town-planning—built on a grid-pattern round two main streets crossing at right-angles, one of which was said to be 100 feet wide. It had magistrates and law-courts after the Greek fashion. The library was a centre of scholarship; the light-house, perhaps with convex mirrors and a lift, one of the marvels of Greek science. But despite this Greek influence the impression left is not of order and reason, but of a vast sprawling cosmopolitan conglomeration, restless and rioting.

> O heavens, what a mob! I can't imagine
> How we're to squeeze through, or how long it'll take—
> An ant-heap's nothing to this hurly-burly.

So the sightseers in the poem, and the city was indeed crowded with Greeks, Jews, Macedonians and Egyptians, and countless others who had come for trade or service. 'This city was an universal nurse,' says a papyrus-scrap, 'every race of men settled in her.' Yet somehow, despite occasional clashes, they came to terms with one another.

This is the story of the Hellenistic Age—Greek culture reaching out through Asia Minor and Syria and Palestine and Egypt, giving them a common language, touching them without quite absorbing them, but enabling the glories of Greek art and the profundities of Greek thought to be transmitted to later generations.

# 5

# ROME

## THE FOUNDATION OF ROME

ROME, the greatest city of the ancient world, 'was not built in a day', and no one knows for certain when it was built. Arnold Toynbee has suggested that civilizations emerge in response to a challenge which is real but not excessive; that is to say that great civilizations do not emerge from arctic snows or desert sands, where the challenge is excessive, nor do they emerge where conditions are too easy and men tend to sit back and stagnate. The great city of Italy sprang up not in the harsh mountains of the north, nor in the comfortable plain of the Po, but in the hill-country of central Italy. Here, on the natural site of a hill-fortress, commanding the lowest crossing of the river Tiber, and a salt route running from the sea to the Apennines, in the years between 1000 and 600 B.C. Rome was founded,

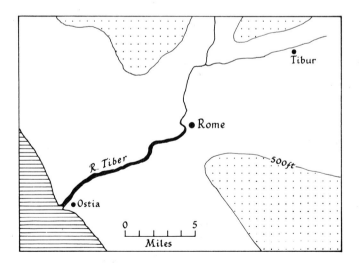

The position of Rome.

64

first as a village, finally as a town: the Romans themselves selected 753 B.C. for the traditional date. Later its centrality in Italy and the growth of a port at the mouth of the Tiber were to be of major importance.

## THE EARLY HISTORY OF ROME

From early times we have little but legend. One of these stories told how Romulus and Remus, two brothers, were thrown as babies into the Tiber, washed ashore and fed by a she-wolf. Later Romulus founded the city. Remus showed his contempt by jumping over the low walls (bad magic, meaning that an enemy would break the walls in the same way) and was killed by his brother. Such stories are not to be taken as history, but we must remember that they touched the imagination of later Romans. The most we can say for certain is that for some centuries Rome was ruled by kings, who replaced the ford by a bridge, developed trade, built a citadel, and started the first big drainage scheme. Then in 510 B.C. the last of the kings was deposed.

Internally the next 250 years was a period of class-conflict between 'patricians' and 'plebeians', the small ruling class and the mass of the citizens. The commons wanted security against arbitrary action, equality of political opportunity, and economic support for the oppressed. The first meant codification of the law, and from the Twelve Tables of 451–450 B.C., the first written code, dates the majestic growth of Roman law. The second meant the opening up of political office. They won this by obtaining their own political assembly and officers, a state within a state. Gradually the other rights were granted, though it remained rare for a commoner to receive high office. The third was met, for the moment, by expansion in Italy and the building of new settlements.

Externally these years saw the expansion of Rome to become supreme in Italy. It was not lightly achieved; there were bitter wars and bitter defeats. Nor was it mere aggression; if Rome was a dragon, she was at least a reluctant dragon. Nor was her rule oppressive; Rome's later enemies, such as Hannibal, were not welcomed as liberators. She held her power by a system of military roads, by the judicious establishment of settlements, and by admitting the towns of Italy either to citizenship of Rome or to terms of alliance.

Part of the Via Appia (312 B.C.), probably the first paved road ever built in the western world; it runs south from Rome to Capua, a distance of over 100 miles, and like all roads built by the Romans is remarkably straight, running directly from one high point to another. Good roads were an essential factor in the efficiency of the civil and military administration, and they proved to be a unifying influence throughout the empire. Remains of these roads can be seen today all over Europe.

## ROME BECOMES A WORLD POWER

The next two hundred years (264–63 B.C.) saw the emergence of Rome as a world power. She was at first an unwilling imperialist, no doubt because the aristocrats saw the difficulty of providing governors for a multitude of appointments outside Italy from their own small numbers. But her destiny was forced upon her. She survived a devastating war with Carthage and the bold genius of Hannibal. Hannibal, brought up to hate Rome, crossed the Alps with an army, including some elephants, smashed the Roman forces in three great battles and occupied Italy for twelve years. But Rome fought back and through Fabius, whom they nicknamed 'Old-Do-Nothing' because he refused to join battle, and the military skill of Scipio she finally won, and found that in the course of the war she had gained Spain. She tried her best to avoid occupying Greece, but only through her intervention could peace be made. The year 146 B.C. saw the wanton destruction of the old enemy Carthage, and of Corinth in Greece, largely through exasperation. In Asia Minor a large territory was bequeathed to Rome by the will of the dying ruler.

Socially the period saw five facts of importance: the dominance of Roman culture by Greece in literature, philosophy, religion, art and architecture; the development of trade, industry and commerce and emergence of the bourgeoisie or commercial middle class; economic oppression by which the small farmers were driven off the land to unemployment in the city, and unsuccessful attempts to put an end to this; selfish discrimination against the Italians outside Rome itself and extortionate government in the overseas provinces; and the fact that Rome's international commitments led to the emergence of the successful general as the dominating figure of power in the state.

## ROMAN GOVERNMENT

The king had been replaced by two officers, of equal powers, elected to serve for one year and to keep a check on each other. These were first called *praetors* ('leaders'), later *consuls* ('co-operators'). Gradually there emerged a system by which an ambitious politician might go through a succession of offices to the highest office of consul. At all points he would be a member of a team and have at least one colleague to check him. The device was typically conservative; from time to time men of little scruple would break through the legal procedure, and disregard the veto of their colleagues. (Julius Caesar ignored his colleague Bibulus, and wits called the year, not the consulate of Bibulus and Caesar, but the consulate of Julius and Caesar.) Only these magistrates were given authority by the state. As the state grew, a clever device allowed a magistrate who had completed his office to serve overseas 'on behalf of the consul', as a *proconsul*. Power lay with the senate, a council of those who had held high office. Finally the officers of the commons, *tribunes* ('group-leaders'), while not possessing authority within the state could use a veto to block action.

## ROMAN CHARACTER

The ideal Roman character showed three qualities. The first they called *virtus*. We get the word 'virtue' from it, but it means rather 'manliness'. In an age when men were farmers and soldiers, it meant 'toughness', endurance and courage. The second quality was *pietas*. Again this means not 'piety' but 'a sense of duty', family solidarity in the narrower sense, patriotism in the wider. The third quality was *gravitas*, 'dignity'.

Many examples can be given of the sort of character the Romans admired. Cincinnatus, the simple farmer, whom they found ploughing his own field when they wanted him as national leader in a time of emergency, is one. C. Popillius Laenas is another. They sent him with a despatch to the king of Syria. Popillius drew a circle in the sand round the king as he read the letter, and forbade him to break the circle before he had given a decisive answer. This was the quality of authority which a Roman soldier was to recognize in Jesus. Even more interesting is M. Atilius Regulus. Regulus was an unsuccessful commander in some early battles with Carthage. He was captured and sent to Rome under oath to return if the Carthaginian prisoners of war in Roman hands were not released. He advised the senate not to release the prisoners, and went back unflinchingly to death by torture. Here, in the courage with which he faced death, in the patriotism which put his country's interests before his own life, and in the dignity with which he bore himself, we have the character the Romans admired.

## CICERO AND CAESAR

The first half of the last century B.C. was an age of interesting personalities, but two for us stand out. Marcus Tullius Cicero (106–43 B.C.) may be taken as the last representative of the old order. A consummate orator and ineffective politician, he tried to preserve the state by allying the aristocrats

CICERO, greatest orator and prose stylist of the Roman world, developed the Latin language into a marvellous instrument both for the precise analysis of a legal brief and for the discursive expression of philosophical ideas. The greater part of his writings has survived, including over a thousand letters which give an invaluable picture of day-to-day life in Rome.

with the middle class, but the power of the generals was too much for him. His more lasting claim to fame lies in his translations of Greek philosophy into Latin. In this way he transmitted Greek thought to the western world, and in so doing gave western Europe her philosophical vocabulary. He was not an original thinker but a clear interpreter: 'I simply provide the words,' he said, 'and I've plenty of those.' Caesar once remarked that he had done less in pushing back the frontiers of empire than Cicero in pushing back the frontiers of thought. We know more about Cicero than anyone until quite modern times through the preservation of more than a thousand of his letters. They are a fascinating record of the times and they reveal the man, vain and vacillating, but companionable, affectionate, and lovable in his weakness.

69

Julius Caesar (*c.* 102–44 B.C.) was a stronger man, who emerged out of the medley of war and civil war which ran through his lifetime, as sole ruler of Rome. Caesar has, even in modern times, been idolized and reviled; each attitude is exaggerated. Like Alexander, he was a brilliant leader in war, with Alexander's daring and swiftness, and his campaigns brought France and Britain within the orbit of Rome. But, like Alexander, he was a constructive statesman as well as a soldier. His measures were remarkable—they include the reform of the calendar, schemes for public works to relieve unemployment, reform of local government, the development of trade, the settlement of Romans overseas, the extension of citizenship, and the introduction into the senate of Gauls from France. This last prompted the ribald lines, sung in the streets:

> Caesar led the Gauls in triumph, to the Senate-House he led;
> And the Gauls took off their trousers, put the toga on instead.

(The toga was the Roman national dress, a long cloth wrapped round the body.) But all these moves, interesting as they are, met the needs of the moment. They were not inspired by any such vision as seems to have moved Alexander. This might have come; perhaps Caesar died too soon. But there are signs that he was tired of life. On 14 March 44 B.C. conversation turned to the best death to die. Caesar looked up from the papers he was signing. 'A sudden one', he said. Next day he was murdered; he was too like an eastern monarch for the supporters of tradition.

LIUS CAESAR, soldier, statesman
d historian, founder of the Roman
pire, has been represented by some
an avid seeker after personal power
d by others as an inspired reformer
th the vision of an Alexander. The
al Caesar was something of both—a
an who valued both power and
iciency, and who, having assumed
preme power, exercised it liberally.
s historical writings are vivid narra-
es of his campaigns, written in the
aightforward prose of the culti-
ted man of action.

71

Roman sculpture in the Augustan age was the highest expression of naturalism, of trueness to life, in art. Yet it is not mere photography. Notice how the sculptor uses the bold curves of the folds of garments to cut across and soften the vertical lines of the procession, as well as to suggest the outline of the limbs beneath. And note how a face or foot, turned outwards, dramatically interrupts the movement from left to right. This part of the Ara Pacis Augustae, an altar with a great plinth decorated by friezes showing files of distinguished Romans, religious processions and sacrificial scenes, gives some idea of Rome's remarkable achievement in realistic sculpture. Towards the end of the reign of Augustus this style degenerated into a traditional academic exercise, and it was not until the time of the Flavian emperors (A.D. 70–96) that sculptors were able to let inspiration override the conventions of the official art. The artists were Greeks.

# AUGUSTUS

Caesar's death gave Rome over to thirteen more years of civil war until his young grandnephew (63 B.C.–A.D. 14) attained the position of supreme dominance which he was to hold for forty-five years. He is best known to us by the name Augustus which he took in 27 B.C. to help to give his position a religious flavour. Augustus was one of those men who, without consummate ability, have a flair for success. He boasted that he found Rome brick and

72

left it marble.  In so saying he was thinking not just of the city buildings, but of the whole structure of empire.  He brought peace, higher standards, responsible legislation, and relief from anxiety.  He gave a feeling of confidence, expressed in the religious revival which he sponsored: the wrath of the gods was annulled.  Temples were restored, religious festivals renewed, and poets and artists set to extol moral values and express a religious view of life.  He exalted the high status of the Roman citizen in a way that Julius had failed to do.  He established the rule of law, and appeared in the courts himself.

AUGUSTUS: A Roman cameo of the (?) first century A.D., set later in the Lotharius cross, part of the treasury of the Holy Roman Empire. The artist has flattered the emperor without losing his characteristic features.

It was said of Pericles of Athens that the constitution was in theory a democracy, in practice the rule of the first citizen. So too Augustus wanted to be the introducer of the best possible condition of affairs, so that the foundations he laid would last (the words are his). He claimed indeed to be restoring the republic—a coin described him as the champion of the *freedom* of the people of Rome. His autocratic power was hedged round and concealed: each part of it was constitutional, but the way it was held was unconstitutional. In no case did he hold higher powers than his colleagues—but he held them for longer and held many at once. The pillars of his power were the authority belonging normally to a proconsul and the right of veto held normally by a tribune. The one gave him command of the armies; by the other he could control what was done politically. The person of the emperor held the empire together. Revered in his lifetime, he was made a god after his death. As with the divine kings of Africa, emperor-worship became important.

His achievement was threefold. He saved Rome alike from eastern tyranny and from ancient forms of party strife, and gave her ordered government. He brought world peace, unity, and the beginning of a sense of 'belonging together'. It was through him that at the birth of Jesus

> No war, or battle's sound
> Was heard the world around;
> The idle spear and shield were high up-hung.

There were frontier wars, but within the empire peace was established. A Greek says that peace had never been so wide; a Jew honours him as 'giver of peace'. He gave to the world the idea of the Eternal City. In this he was well served by his greatest poet Vergil, who had a magnificent sense of the destiny of Rome:

> Others may better plead the cause, may compass heaven's face,
> And mark it out, and tell the stars, their rising and their place;
> But thou, O Roman, look to it the folks of earth to sway;
> For this shall be thine handicraft, peace on the world to lay,
> To spare the weak, to wear the proud by constant weight of war.

# THE AUGUSTAN AGE

The reign of Augustus marks the high point of Roman culture. The Romans never claimed cultural originality. They were content to allow that to the Greeks. But in borrowing they adapted, and produced a new synthesis. The end of the Republic had seen the intense majestic genius of Lucretius, and the intense love-poetry of Catullus. Only one Augustan poet could rival their intensity—Propertius. The Augustans were delicate, refined, balanced. Vergil achieved a balance which has never been surpassed. Horace produced the appearance of spontaneously happy results by taking infinite pains, an amiable man and a good companion even today. Ovid, the poet of wit, wrought near-perfect epigrams in a limited medium and told vivid stories in verse.

The same is to be seen in sculpture, though here the actual artists were Greeks not Romans. Under the Romans they developed portraiture to a fine art. The master-work of the Augustan Age is, however, the Altar of Peace, the Ara Pacis Augustae, at Rome. This was built to celebrate the safe return of the emperor from France and Spain. Noble panels showed figures of myth—Aeneas sacrificing, and Romulus and Remus suckled by the wolf—and of symbol—Rome at peace with her armour laid aside, and Mother Earth in all her fertility; and a frieze depicted a religious procession with the emperor and his family, the religious officers and the ordinary citizens.


# THE INDIAN SUMMER OF THE ANTONINES

At one point Augustus's political shrewdness deserted him: he insisted on hereditary succession. Thrice in the first century A.D. Rome nearly foundered when a megalomaniac inherited the throne; fortunately a single individual at the centre could not wholly overthrow long traditions of government. Then, at the very end of the century, a new principle came into being, perhaps by the accident of childlessness: each emperor adopted the best possible successor, and a century of prosperity dawned.

Edward Gibbon, the scholarly and sarcastic historian of Rome's decline, paid eloquent tribute to this era:

If a man were called to fix the period in the history of the world during which the condition of the human race was most happy and prosperous, he would without hesitation name that which elapsed from the death of Domitian to the accession of Commodus. The vast extent of the Roman Empire was governed by absolute power, under the guidance of virtue and wisdom. The armies were restrained by the firm but gentle hand of four successive emperors, whose characters and authority commanded involuntary respect. The forms of the civil administration were carefully preserved by Nerva, Trajan, Hadrian and the Antonines, who delighted in the image of liberty, and were pleased with considering themselves as the accountable ministers of the laws. Such princes deserved the honour of restoring the republic, had the Romans of their days been capable of enjoying a rational freedom.

We may note four things about this period.

In the reign of Trajan (b. A.D. 53, ruled 98–117) the empire reached its widest extent, embracing Rumania and Mesopotamia.

Though there were wars on the frontiers, a larger area of the world's surface enjoyed a longer period of untroubled peace than probably ever before or since. Travel was swift and safe. Hadrian (b. A.D. 76, ruled 117–38) made

Officers and standard-bearers of a Roman army marching across the Danube on a bridge of boats. A relief from Trajan's column, erected to celebrate his victorious campaigns against the Dacians in what is now Rumania.

The frontiers of the Roman Empire were guarded by systems of fortifications and entrenchments. Hadrian's Wall, which extended across the north of Britain from Bowness in Cumberland to Wallsend in Northumberland, was a turf or stone wall about 20 feet high and 6 to 8 feet across, strengthened at intervals by fortified towers and look-out posts. To the north of the wall a deep ditch was dug where there was no natural obstacle. Sentry duty at the wall, remote from civilization and the sunny climate of Italy, must have been one of the less popular assignments of the Roman soldier. Much of the wall still stands, but not all in as good a state of preservation as the stretch shown here.

three long journeys to distant parts of the empire, and twenty years later an orator announces: 'Everyone, Greek or non-Greek, can easily travel to whatever destination he chooses; neither the Cilician Gates' (a distant mountain-pass in Asia) 'nor the tracks of the deserts need make him afraid.'

Law was developed, and made more humane. Notable is the principle that law deals with intention as well as action (a modern example is the distinction

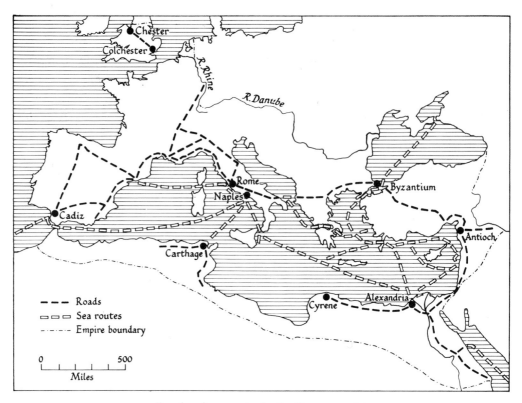

Land and sea routes in the Roman world.

between murder, manslaughter and accidental death); and the better treatment of slaves (henceforth a master who killed his slave was liable to a charge of murder).

In general it was an age of benevolent paternalism; that is to say there was government of the people, for the people, but not by the people.

## MARCUS AURELIUS

Of the rulers of the second century we know best Marcus Aurelius (b. A.D. 121, ruled 161–80). He is a fascinating but pathetic figure, who has left us a series of notebooks in which he jotted down his thoughts while campaigning on the Danube. He was a philosopher; in him Plato's dream of a philosopher-king

78

MARCUS AURELIUS on horseback, the statue on the Capitol at Rome.

became real. But although he was brought up a Stoic, the notebooks show a man uncertain what to believe, and his face in his statues is weak, not strong. His reign was disastrous; it was, says one historian, the end of the ancient world. He could not be held responsible for the plague which ravaged his people, nor entirely for wars which came on him from outside. But he was responsible for making the state so bankrupt that he had to sell the crown-jewels and debase the coinage; he was responsible for leaving his people in the grip of bureaucracy; he was responsible for allowing persecution of his Christian subjects; he was above all responsible for insisting that his worthless son Commodus should succeed him, so undoing the work of a century.


## THE DISASTERS OF THE THIRD CENTURY

In the 104 years which follow the death of Marcus there were twenty-nine emperors and innumerable pretenders; in the fifteen years of Gallienus' reign alone we can name eighteen, and tradition tells of a dozen more. This is enough to show the turmoil and uncertainty. Said Gibbon: 'The rapid and perpetual transitions from the cottage to the throne, and from the throne to the grave, might have amused an indifferent philosopher, were it possible for a philosopher to remain indifferent amidst the general calamities of mankind.' These emperors came from the most varied parts of the empire and all classes of society, from Africa to Arabia, from peasants to princes. The army were the king-makers; at one point they actually put the empire up for auction to the highest bidder; the millionaire who was foolish enough to buy it paid with his life a few days later.

During this tragic period one event merits special mention. In A.D. 212 the emperor Caracalla decreed that virtually all the free inhabitants of the Roman empire should have Roman citizenship—the story of Paul in the book of Acts reminds us how much this was prized. The measure, fulfilling much that had gone before, gave the empire greater unity, though it could not stave off the pressure from outside.

Eventually resistance stiffened. Aurelian (ruled A.D. 270–5) brought back discipline, tempered with mercy. Soldiers were forbidden to gamble or drink, to damage crops, steal sheep or oppress civilians. 'Their wealth should be collected from the spoil of the enemy, not the tears of the provincial.'

Aurelian was a skilful commander, a strong personality and something of a statesman; his reign saw the building of a mighty wall round Rome which stands today. He also found a religion for his empire in the worship of the sun, which gives life and shines impartially on all. The new temple was dedicated on 25 December A.D. 274, the 'birthday' of the unconquered sun, a date the Christians borrowed and still use.

## DIOCLETIAN

Ten years later the throne reached the hands of one of the most remarkable men of antiquity, Diocletian, a farmer's son with a genius for organization. The empire was too large for one man to handle in time of crisis. He divided it into four, two portions to be administered by senior emperors called

Reconstruction of the palace of Diocletian on the Adriatic coast at Split, in Yugoslavia. Note the famous octagon.

'Augustus', two by juniors called 'Caesar'. The term of office was to be ten years, when an 'Augustus' would retire, a 'Caesar' would be promoted 'Augustus', and a new 'Caesar' appointed. There were four (possibly more) senior administrative officers, thirteen regions with their governors and 116 provinces with their District Commissioners. The emperor became more remote, but the government became more efficient. In addition an astonishing edict of A.D. 301 attempted to meet economic crisis by fixing maximum prices throughout the empire for every conceivable commodity from cabbages to gold embroidery and every conceivable service from that of the unskilled labourer to that of the barrister.

## THE BREAK-UP OF THE ROMAN EMPIRE

Diocletian retired, when his time came, to plant cabbages in Yugoslavia. His scheme shuddered and broke, though many of its details remained. Under Constantine, as we shall see, Christianity reached the throne, and the centre of empire moved to the east. The western, Latin world strained on for another century, till in A.D. 410 Rome fell to invaders from outside, and the glory that had belonged to the empire turned to the church.

The decline of Rome has been variously explained. Some accounts are personal. If only Julius Caesar had been murdered earlier—or later. If only Trajan had not extended the frontiers too far—or Hadrian reduced them. If only Marcus Aurelius had not insisted on his son's succeeding him. Some are political. Rome, it is suggested, failed to hold together empire and self-government. Or free enterprise decayed into bureaucracy. Some are military. Movements in western China drove the central Asiatics westwards and brought against Rome armies too strong to repel. Or again, the army ought never to have been reduced in size. Some are medical and biological, and blame malaria or plague or the mixing of the races. Some are economic and blame the exhaustion of the soil, changes of climate, the use of slaves, the failure to develop industry. Some are sociological, and blame the vice of the people, or the influence of the Christians in opposing war.

Some of these suggestions contradict others. Some can be shown to be inadequate: there was, for instance, no soil-exhaustion in Egypt. Historical truth is rarely simple, and the answer probably lies in a combination of several of these.

Roman city life. A reconstruction of a street of apartment buildings (*insulae*) at the Porticus Margaritaria on the Sacra Via. The buildings are remarkably like those of a present-day European town.

A triumph of Roman engineering skill: the Pont du Gard, at Nîmes, in France. This great three-fold bridge over the river Gard was an aqueduct as well as a road-bridge. The watercourse ran along the upper level.

# WHAT ROME GAVE THE WORLD

Rome gave to the world unity. It made of this mixed, muddled, varied world of ours a single state. The seas were free of pirates, the lands were spanned by splendid roads on which 60 miles a day was normal, and 180 possible. There were no passports, no visas, no forms to fill. The Romans were tolerant of others; one emperor put in his chapel the image of Jesus alongside the heroes of Rome and Greece. They had a genius for assimilation. Here is a Roman historian writing of a governor of the wild and distant island of Britain. 'He trained the sons of the chiefs in the liberal arts and expressed a preference for British natural ability over the trained skill of the Gauls. The result was that in place of a distaste for the Latin language came a passion to command it. In the same way, our national dress came into favour and the toga was everywhere to be seen.' He goes on to describe how the Britons accepted baths and banquets as a part of 'civilization'.

The Romans did this by a system of double citizenship. A man would be a citizen of his local town and (by the third century) of the whole empire, of St Albans and Rome. This gave him a local loyalty and a universal loyalty. But the Romans sought to break down the loyalty given to a nation-state. Loyalty to England or France they thought divisive; and the history of Europe since shows that they were right. In modern terms they would encourage a man to think himself, say, a citizen of Accra and the United Nations, but not of Ghana.

The result can be seen in the praise given to pagan Rome by the Christian poet Prudentius. 'Peoples discordant in speech, kingdoms diverse in culture, God willed to unite, God would submit to one rule, and God would have them in harmonious union, submitted to a gentle sway.... There is no union fit for Christ unless one mind unite all the nations together.'

We of the twentieth century have not yet recaptured the vision, still less the reality.

# 6

# CHRISTIANITY

## JESUS OF NAZARETH

ALTHOUGH we date our era from the traditional birth of Jesus (B.C. means 'Before Christ', and A.D. or Anno Domini 'In the year of the Lord'), Jesus was probably born in fact a year or two B.C. His mother Mary was wife to Joseph, the village carpenter of Nazareth in Palestine. His name is the same as that borne by the great national leader who brought the Hebrews into their promised land. Joseph seems to have died early, and Jesus probably followed the trade of carpenter until his brothers and sisters were grown up. Then, at the age of thirty, he set out on a mission as a wandering preacher, accompanied by a group of fishermen and others. His gifts of healing came into prominence at this time. At first the mission was overwhelmingly successful. The crowds flocked to him. Then he offended the authorities; he was unorthodox and outspoken. The crowds began to straggle and fall away. But he was still a power to reckon with, and in going into Jerusalem he knew that he was going into danger. Forced into a position where he could do nothing else without being untrue to his faith, he allowed himself to be arrested and executed; his death is usually dated to A.D. 33.

## THE KINGDOM OF GOD

Jesus's teaching centred on the Kingdom of God, the reign or authority of God. We have seen that the Jews were waiting for the Messiah, God's anointed king, to set up a kingdom of peace and justice. Jesus proclaimed that the kingdom of God was at hand, growing as a tree shoots up in the tropical rains, so fast that you scarcely notice it until it overshadows you.

JERUSALEM. In the foreground is the Temple area.

Man does not build the kingdom; it grows of itself; he accepts it, enters it. This is another way of saying that God is at work in the world; man has only to learn to work with him. The kingdom is in the first place within; Jesus is thinking of Jeremiah's words that there must be a new covenant in the hearts of men. God is king where men obey his authority. But this obedience must be worked out in life. The man who has God as king has a changed attitude to Caesar. So Jesus was, and was regarded as, a revolutionary.

## JESUS'S MORAL TEACHING

Jesus attacked the Pharisees of his day for being concerned with outward acts rather than inward character, like people who wash the outside of a cup and leave the part they drink from full of germs, and for being so concerned for small things that they missed things which matter more, like a man who strains all the insects out of his drink and swallows a camel without noticing it, or a man who tries to get a speck of sawdust out of a fellow-worker's eye without noticing a plank sticking in his own. (In these Jesus gave comically exaggerated examples to drive his point home.) A sensible rule, going back to the Ten Commandments, said that each week there should be a day of rest. Jesus offended the Pharisees by healing ill people on that day; he thought it more important to do good than to keep the rule. So again he said that it was not enough not to commit murder; men must get rid of the attitude of mind from which murder comes.

CHRIST as a young man teaching. A Roman statuette of *c.* A.D. 350.

Jesus was not trying to do away with the old ways, rather to deepen them. His genius lay not so much in saying something new as in selecting what really mattered from all that had been said before. Thus he reduced the whole Old Testament to two commandments—love God and love your neighbour; both are found within the Old Testament. Yet his single-minded emphasis on love, a distant echo of Hosea, was in its strength new. His followers were to show love in all relations of life, public and personal, and towards all, to God, to one another as the cement of their fellowship, to their neighbours, and to enemies like the hated Roman imperialists or the footpads who lay in secluded parts of the road. This love meant a refusal to resist evil with evil, and a constant seeking of the deepest well-being of the person concerned.

## THE MESSIAH

Palestine was an occupied country, with its quislings or collaborators (the 'publicans' who collected the taxes for the Romans) and its resistance movement (the 'zealots'). In this context those who were waiting for the Messiah came to think of him as a resistance leader who would bring war against the Romans as the way of setting up the Kingdom. Jesus claimed to be the Messiah, but he refused to raise the flag of violent revolt; it is possible that the misguided follower who betrayed him was trying to force his hand and drive him into open war. But Jesus said that the Messiah was the same as the suffering servant of Deutero-Isaiah's poems. He too believed that the way forward was through suffering, and death was not the end; and instead of resisting arrest, he suffered the death of a criminal.

## PENTECOST

Jesus had had twelve intimate followers, their leader a fisherman called Simon, whom he nicknamed Peter or Rock. He had plainly hoped that they would stand with him at the last, but they deserted him in fear. For seven weeks the authorities heard nothing of them. Then at the Jewish festival of Pentecost when the city was crowded with pilgrims, they were uplifted by a power greater than themselves, as they said, and came out into the open. The message they proclaimed was this: 'Jesus of Nazareth was shown by his life to be a man of God; he was killed by lawless men; God raised him from the dead so that he lives despite death; he has sent the Spirit of Holiness to inspire us; repent and be baptized every one of you in the name of Jesus Christ for the forgiveness of your sins, and you shall receive the gift of the Holy Spirit.' The most important things here are the belief that Jesus had risen from the dead, and the belief that God sent his Holy Spirit to inspire the faithful.


## PAUL

The new sect came to be called the Christians, the followers of the Christ or Messiah. From the first they met opposition, which soon developed into persecution, and one of their outstanding leaders, named Stephen, was killed by stoning. His faith and courage struck deep into the heart of one of the persecutors, a young man named Saul. Saul did what people uncertain of themselves commonly do, showing still more vigour in persecution, but on a journey to Damascus he had a vision which finally persuaded him that the Christians were right, and he became an enthusiastic Christian, taking the Christian name of Paul. From then his life reads like a story-book adventure.

Five times I have received at the hands of the Jews forty lashes less one; three times I have been beaten with rods; once I was stoned; three times I have been shipwrecked; a night and a day I have been adrift at sea; on frequent journeys, in danger from rivers, danger from robbers, danger from my own people, danger from Gentiles, danger in the city, danger in the wilderness, danger at sea, danger from false brethren; in toil and hardship, through many a sleepless night, in hunger and thirst, often without food, in cold and exposure.

Paul's importance lies in the fact that, though himself a Jew, he saw Christianity not as a sect within Judaism but as a world religion. He himself preached through Asia Minor, Greece, Italy (where he was taken into custody) and possibly Spain, and gave the impulse to the spread of Christianity through the Roman Empire.

Paul is an important but difficult thinker. To him the person of the Christ came to have mystical meaning. He had wrestled to obey the moral laws of the Old Testament, and the effort drove him to despair. Then he came to see God at work in Jesus, and to feel that it was better to trust in God than to

89

PAUL preaching at Athens. Design for a tapestry by Raphael.

We have no picture drawn during their lifetime of the apostles and the first generation of Christians. Our ideas are largely drawn from the art of later times, above all the art of the great Italian painters of the Renaissance.

This is one of Raphael's great compositions. The apostle dominates the scene, a simple upright figure, his pose echoed by the pillars in the background. His out-thrust arms break this pattern of vertical lines, as his voice breaks the silence of his listeners. A statue in the background seems to balance his figure; between the two is a semicircle of listening figures in poses of rapt attention, surprise, and doubt.

In the background is a circular temple very like the architecture of Raphael's contemporary Bramante.

trust in man. The Christian can become one with Jesus—or, rather, the Christian is the person who does become one with Jesus; it is now not a matter of his own striving, but Jesus Christ, risen from the dead, lives in him.

'The secret is simply this: Christ in you! Yes, Christ in you bringing with him the hope of all the glorious things to come.' This is Paul's cry of triumphant certainty.


## THE CHURCH

The Christians were organized in small communities or churches. From the first they practised a simple form of communism, sharing all things. Women and men met on equal terms and called one another 'brother' and 'sister'. Once a week they joined in a common meal, the Supper of Love. They remembered how Jesus just before his betrayal shared a common meal with his disciples, and broke bread and poured out wine to show how his body was to be broken and his blood poured out. They now took part in the Eucharist, or Thanksgiving, sharing bread and wine, and opening their lives to the power which they believed to come from the sacrifice of their Master.

The churches were well organized. Each community had its own elders, presbyters or priests, and over a church or a group of churches would be set a superintendent or bishop. This organization gave the whole Christian body great strength. Similarly the methods of the churches were well ordered and thorough: they distinguished between the *preaching* in which they reached out to tell strangers their fundamental faith so as to bring them in, and the *teaching* whereby they instructed those who responded in the details of the Christian way of life.


## THE ROMANS AND THE CHRISTIANS

We have two interesting accounts of the Christians by Roman authors from the beginning of the second century A.D.: Tacitus is writing of the great fire at Rome in A.D. 64, which some people supposed that Nero started.

To suppress this rumour, Nero fabricated scapegoats—and punished with every refinement the notoriously depraved Christians (as they were popularly called). Their originator, Christ, had been executed in Tiberius' reign by the governor of Judaea, Pontius Pilatus. But in spite of this temporary setback the deadly superstition had broken out afresh, not only in Judaea (where the mischief had started) but even in Rome. All degraded and shameful practices collect and flourish in the capital.

And here is Pliny, as governor of Asia Minor, writing to the emperor Trajan. He is speaking of some ex-Christians who had recanted.

They affirmed, however, that the whole of their guilt, or their error, was that they were in the habit of meeting on a certain fixed day before it was light, when they sang in alternate verses a hymn to Christ, as to a god, and bound themselves by a solemn oath, not to any wicked deeds, but never to commit any fraud, theft or adultery, never to falsify their word, nor deny a trust when they should be called upon to deliver it up; after which it was their custom to separate, and then reassemble to partake of food— but food of an ordinary and innocent kind.

The Christians were for nearly 300 years the object of spasmodic persecution. There were various reasons for this. When the Christians, in taking the bread and wine of the Eucharist, talked of 'eating the body and drinking the

A Roman martyr of A.D. 258: St Lawrence, deacon of Pope Sixtus II. It was the deacon's function to keep the sacred books and to read the Gospel during services; so Lawrence is shown here bearing an open gospel. The fire and gridiron refer to the way he is said to have died. The open cupboard contains the four separate books of the gospel.

From a mosaic in the mausoleum of Galla Placidia at Ravenna.

blood of the Lord', they were accused of being cannibals. Their talk of love, combined with the freedom of women, led those outside to accuse them of immoral behaviour. They spread among the lower classes, and the Roman government feared them as a secret society. Later, their refusal to worship the emperor made people think them unpatriotic, and this belief was strengthened by the refusal of many of them to take part in war. The truth is that they had a higher loyalty than Rome, and Rome could not tolerate this.

## WHY CHRISTIANITY SPREAD

Despite persecution the Christians increased in number, and we can see some of the reasons for this.

They had a message of hope for the oppressed. If man did not care for

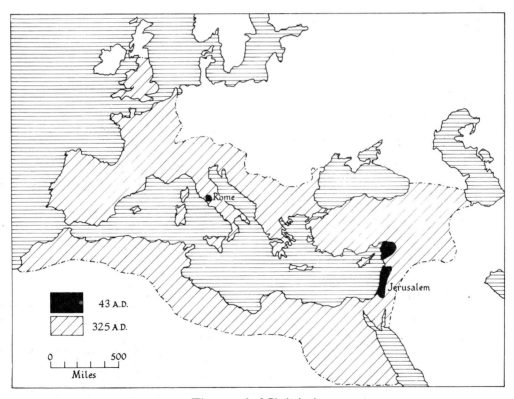

The spread of Christianity.

him, God cared. In the church he found that he mattered; the man whom the Roman noble thrust on one side found himself the equal of any.

In a world of sudden death the preaching that Christ had risen, that God could raise a human from death to everlasting life, gave a new meaning to life on earth as well as hope for the future.

The organization of the churches enabled them to withstand persecution. Some fell away, but most remained strong.

The honour given to women also gave them strength, for a determined woman is a great source of power.

The person of Jesus was historical (unlike the gods of legend), vivid and magnetic.

The way of love was something new. Those who stood outside the church said in admiration, 'How these Christians love one another!' The spirit of forgiveness they showed to their persecutors pointed a similar lesson.

The courage and faith of those who were killed struck home to those who watched. We may think of the woman who in her trial uttered with calm dignity just four words. When asked 'Guilty or not guilty?' she replied '*Christiana sum*', 'I am a Christian'. When condemned to death she said '*Deo gratias*', 'Thanks be to God'. She bore a cruel death with fortitude. The blood of the martyrs—the word 'martyr' means 'witness'—was the seed of the church.

In general, as T. R. Glover once said, the early Christians 'out-thought, out-lived and out-died' the pagans of the time.


## CONSTANTINE

Even before the end of the first century A.D. it seems that a relative of the emperor was converted to Christianity. By the fourth century we find the emperor himself a convert. Constantine (ruled A.D. 306–37) was a curious person. His family, though tolerant towards Christianity, had been sun-worshippers. When he was marching to secure supreme power at Rome in A.D. 312 he saw a cross of light superimposed on the sun—a rare but known phenomenon—and the words came to him 'Triumph in this'. He put on his standards the *Chi-rho* symbol, the first two letters of the name Christ in Greek, and he did triumph. But he did not immediately become a Christian;

CONSTANTINE. A fragment of the huge statue once in the Basilica Constantini on the Forum, built 314–20. The statue was designed to be impressive rather than lifelike. Does its size and watchfulness indicate that the monarch wished to be thought of as a god?

indeed he was baptized only on his death-bed. He continued to issue coins in honour of Hercules, Mars, Jupiter and the Sun (coins in those days were used for propaganda). The Christian symbol had come to him from the sun, and Christ and the sun became blurred in his mind. But he showed great favour to the Christians. It was now fashionable to be a Christian; non-Christians were at a disadvantage, and place-seekers and hypocrites joined the church. Constantine himself was not insincere. He became increasingly interested and increasingly committed, and although not baptized, took part in some of the religious discussions of the time: so was born the dangerous idea that the head of the state is lord of the church. Constantine did not really understand what he was doing. His god was the god of power, never the god of love. The result was as much that Christianity was changed for the worse as that the empire was changed for the better. Constantine is one of the great makers of history, but he is one of the least attractive of them.

## DISPUTE AND DISAGREEMENT

When a faith is fresh, those who hold it are so thrilled that they go out to proclaim it rather than sit back to think about it. Later, thought sets in, rightly. As the Christians began to think they began to disagree and to quarrel. The words which the pagans once spoke in admiration, 'How these Christians love one another!', they now spoke in sarcasm. It is foolish to speak as if ideas did not matter and these disputes were empty; ideas do matter. Nevertheless, the bitterness of the disagreement and the exclusion from Christian fellowship of men of goodwill and upright life, because of intellectual differences honestly held, seem far from the spirit of Jesus.

One important but difficult doctrine which emerged is that of the Trinity. According to this God is in his inner being three, Father, Son and Holy Spirit, while remaining one—three *persons* and one *substance*, 'Three in One and One in Three'. God had been known in the traditions of the Jews; as the Christians looked back at the life of Jesus they came to believe that they could see there God in a human life; as they looked on their experience of the Holy Spirit they came to feel that they were being gripped by God. But this, they believed, was not merely the way in which man experienced God; it expressed something in the nature of God himself. Centuries later, when the

Eastern or Orthodox Church separated from the Western or Catholic, it was over their understanding of the Trinity. The Catholics said that the Holy Spirit 'proceeded' from the Father and the Son, the Orthodox from the Father only. But this difference, though the point of quarrel, was only one of many; ultimately it was the difference between Latin and Greek culture which mattered, and the rival claims of Rome and Constantinople to rule the world.

Another important doctrine concerned the person of Jesus. The Christians came to claim that Jesus was fully human and fully divine, fully man and fully God. The great quarrel of the fourth century was between those who, led by Athanasius, held that Jesus was 'of the same being' as God and those who, led by Arius, wanted to say 'of similar being'. The two words differ in Greek by one letter, but they express a real difference. Athanasius held the day, though Arius' supporters were influential throughout the fourth century.

## THE MONKS

Jesus's teaching contained much about the dangers of riches, and this led some Christians to give away all their possessions and live the simple life. At first they lived within the fellowship of the Church. About A.D. 300 there rose a new movement in Egypt. Some Christians would give up all they had and retire alone to the desert to live a life of solitary prayer and suffering. The dangers of this were noted by one of the great leaders of Christian history, Basil of Caesarea (c. 330–79). He and his friend Gregory felt that neither the life wholly within the 'world', nor that wholly outside it, was right:

> Long was the inward strife, till ended thus:
> I saw, when men lived in the fretful world,
> They vantaged other men, but missed the while
> The calmness, and the pureness of their hearts.
> Those who retired held an uprighter post,
> And raised their eyes with quiet strength to heaven;
> Yet served self only, unfraternally.
> And so, 'twixt these and those, I struck my path,
> To meditate with the free solitary,
> Yet to live secular, and serve mankind.

The monastery of Baramus, in the Wa[di]
Natrun in Egypt, founded in A.D. 330.

Holy men had lived lives of contemplatio[n,]
prayer, self-denial and withdrawal from t[he]
world before Christian times. Early Christia[ns]
too abstained from marriage, from meat a[nd]
intoxicating drink, and devoted themselves [to]
prayer and works of charity. But at first it w[as]
in their own homes. In about A.D. 270 t[he]
Egyptian Christian Anthony withdrew fro[m]
the world, and became a hermit, living alo[ne]
in the desert. The fame of his piety broug[ht]
others to live in the same manner in the cav[es]
and rocks near him, and to seek his leadershi[p.]
When he agreed to organize the life of all the[se]
hermits early in the fourth century he becam[e]
the founder of Christian monasticism. Th[e]
monks in the later monasteries of the Wa[di]
Natrun lived in more organized communitie[s,]
more like the great monastic orders whic[h]
began to be founded when monasticis[m]
reached the Latin West. Athanasius too[k]
two monks to Rome in A.D. 340. The gre[at]
founder of western monasticism w[as]
Benedict, who founded the Benedictine orde[r]
at Monte Cassino in Italy. It was the monk[s]
who throughout the Dark Ages after th[e]
break-up of the Roman Empire preserve[d]
the artistic, literary and educational heritag[e]
of Rome.

Basil encouraged Christians to retire, but as monks in communities, where they could keep habits of industrious service to others. His work was taken up in the West by Benedict of Nursia (c. 480–550) with notable results.

## TELEMACHUS

The way in which a single Christian might change history is shown in the achievement of a monk named Telemachus. We know nothing else about him, and even his name is not quite certain. One of the scandals of ancient Rome was the gladiatorial 'games'. Men were forced to butcher one another for the sport of spectators. Some humane Romans, such as the philosopher Seneca, protested. But Seneca, as regent for Nero, held the supreme power in the Roman world without doing anything to abolish the shows. Three hundred years later one of the most cultured pagans of the day brought some Saxon gladiators from the north at great expense to celebrate his son's birthday.

98

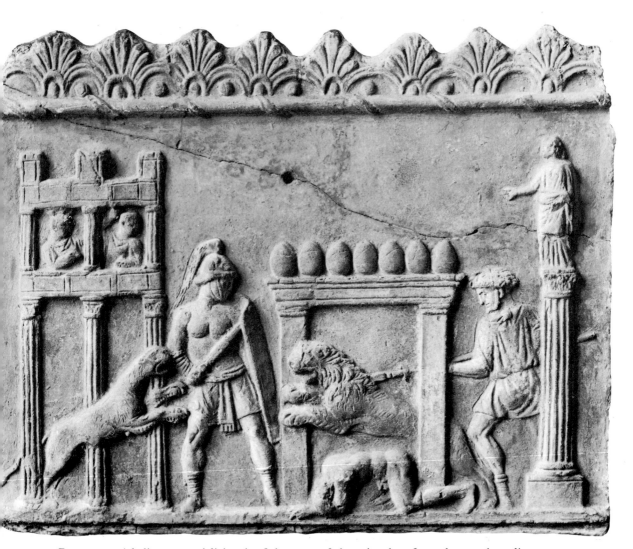

BESTIARII (gladiators specializing in fights with animals) in a Roman circus. One has been wounded and crouches on the ground. While two others meet the attack of a lion, one of them is taken from the rear by a lioness. Above, the spectators. The seven 'eggs' indicate the total number of acts in the day's games. One was removed after each act.

They killed themselves rather than fight; and the Roman, normally a humane and gentle man, has only words of bitterness. Constantine, a Christian on the throne, did nothing to abolish the shows, nor did his successors. Then, on 1 January 404, this monk Telemachus went into the arena and stood between the fighters and bade them cease in the name of Jesus Christ. He was cut down on the spot amid the jeers of the crowd whose cruel sport he had dared to interrupt. Yet his death bore fruit, and that was the last gladiatorial show held in Rome.

Fathers of the Latin Church. Gregory the Great, Augustine and Silvester. Twelfth-century mosaics in the cathedral of Cefalu, Sicily.

# AUGUSTINE

Augustine (354–430) is in some ways the last great figure of the ancient world and the first of the medieval. He ranks with Origen (*c.* 185–254) as one of the two great minds of the first centuries of Christianity. He was brought up a Christian but did not long remain one. A book of Cicero led him back to serious thinking, and the influence of his pious mother Monica and Ambrose the great bishop of Milan gradually led him back to the faith he had left. One day, sitting in a garden, he seemed to hear the words 'Pick it up and read'. He picked up a Bible lying near and read: 'Let us conduct ourselves becomingly as in the day, not in revelling and drunkenness, not in debauchery and licentiousness, not in quarrelling and jealousy. But put on the Lord Jesus Christ, and make no provision for the flesh to gratify its desires.' From that moment the return was complete. Augustine has left us a fascinating record of his early struggles, viewed through the reflections of later life, in his *Confessions*.

Augustine became bishop of Hippo in North Africa. Much of his life was spent in three disputes, first with those who believed that there is an evil power in the world alongside God and that this physical world is essentially evil; then with those who did not want to receive back into the Church those who under persecution had denied their faith; then with those who held that man is by his own nature capable of doing right. In answering these Augustine built a masterly and majestic system of theology. To the first he said that God was the creator of all things and saw that they were good; to the second that the Church is holy because of its purposes, not the character of its members, which it is not for us to judge; to the third that it is only by the grace of God that we can do right. Unfortunately he also came to believe that it was right to call in the police to deal with those who did not accept the true faith of the Church, and the effect of this was harmful.

Augustine's greatest book, a large work entitled *The City of God*, was called out by the fall of Rome in 410. Some had blamed Christianity for the disaster. Augustine champions Christianity and says that there are and always have been two cities, the city of the world, whose citizens may prosper in this life but not beyond, and the city of God, whose citizens may suffer in this life but who are ultimately right.

arly Christian symbolism. The *Chi-rho* onogram of Christ is contained within a ctor's laurel wreath, which hangs from the ak of an imperial eagle and is supported by o doves, symbols of the soul. These stand the arms of an upright cross, flanked by e two soldiers who guarded the tomb of e crucified Christ. The whole is therefore mbolic of the triumphant Resurrection. It mes from a Roman sarcophagus.

# THE CHARACTER OF CHRISTIANITY

If we are asked what Christianity had given to the world, we might single out three things.

First, in the person of Jesus those of other faiths and of none, as well as Christians, have seen a standard of what man can be, an example and an inspiration.

Secondly, the Christian teaching that in Jesus God became man ('The Word became flesh' says one Christian writing: the doctrine is called the Incarnation) led Christians to see this life and this world not as something to be escaped from or merely accepted or exploited but as something to be changed and redeemed. Christianity, of all the great religions, has had the finest record of social service, as the work of the missions may remind us. From the early days Christians went out to help the needy in times of crisis, to build schools and hospitals, and if they did not abolish slavery in the ancient world, at least they did in the modern. They stopped the gladiatorial shows; they stopped the killing of unwanted children.

Thirdly, the Christian way of love was something new, and the Christians themselves have not yet realized or recaptured its full meaning.

# 7

# BYZANTIUM

## THE EARLY HISTORY OF BYZANTIUM

FOR a thousand years Byzantium, founded as a Greek colony in 667 B.C., gave no promise of its future glory. It was a fishing-town, wealthy enough for the harbour where the fish were caught to be called the Golden Horn; the Romans speak highly of fish-pickle from Byzantium. In addition revenue was got by taxing ships which passed carrying corn from the Black Sea to the Mediterranean. The situation was always splendid. Byzantium stands on a headland at the meeting of three waterways; that to the north leads to the Black Sea, that to the south-west to the Mediterranean, and the angle between the two is cut by the magnificent harbour of the Golden Horn. These waterways, together with the Muslim minarets, make the beauty of the modern city of Istanbul; they have always been the secret of the power and prosperity of the place.

One curious byway of history is worth recording. In 340 B.C. the people of Byzantium repelled an attack from Macedon, and attributed their success to the favour of the moon-goddess. They put on their coins the symbol of the crescent and the star, and it was from this source that it passed to Islam.

## THE CITY OF CONSTANTINE

By A.D. 300 the centre of gravity within the Roman empire had shifted from the west to the east. From that side came military danger, and two emperors had died on the northern and eastern frontiers; it seems that events in western China set up a chain of disturbance in central Asia which gradually made itself felt on the other side of the continent. The art, literature, thought and culture of the empire were Greek. The religions of the east had increasingly caught

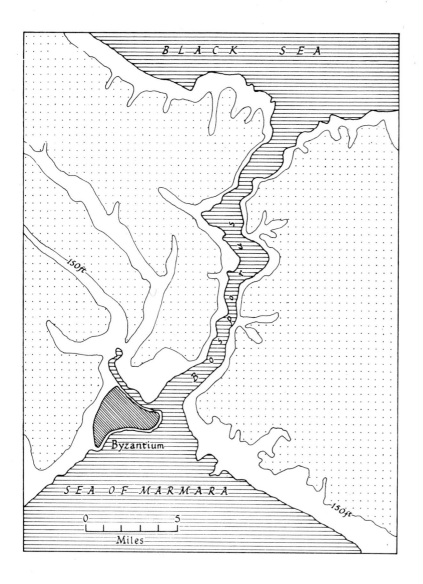

The position of Byzantium.

the imagination of the people; Christianity was only one of many cults which swept through Rome. Above all, agriculture had declined in Italy; it remained prosperous in the east.

So when Constantine looked for a new capital for his now Christian empire, he looked eastwards. He toyed with Troy, then chose a better site at Byzantium. On 8 November 324, the wall was begun, on 11 May 330 the city was solemnly dedicated. It is clear that it was intended as a Christian city, and pagan rites were forbidden, though Fortune and the Unconquered Sun were still honoured, and the statue of the emperor wearing the rayed crown of the sun-god (made, as he believed, from the nails with which Jesus was crucified) was revered by Christian and pagan alike.

Constantine intended his capital to be called New Rome, but the name Constantine's City, Constantino-polis, stuck instead.

## THE HISTORY OF THE BYZANTINE EMPIRE

Until recently the history of New Rome has received harsh treatment from historians. To Gibbon it was a 'tedious and uniform tale of weakness and misery', and Lecky wrote: 'Of that Byzantine Empire the universal verdict of history is that it constitutes, without a single exception, the most thoroughly base and despicable form that civilization has yet assumed.' Modern studies have revised that verdict. Yet the details of the history scarcely matter. The record of wars, victories and defeats soon palls. The great fortress stood shock after shock. It stood when the western empire fell. It stood against the Persians; it stood against the Goths. For a moment it held Africa and Spain: then they fell away before the Muslim armies. It stood against the Slav, and it stood against the Arab in the danger time of A.D. 717–18. It was ironical that it should fall to the Catholic Christian Crusaders on 13 April 1204; the pope of the day condemned the deed and applauded the result. From that moment it was doomed. For the next 250 years it dragged on, a pitiful remnant of empire. On 29 May 1453 the city was taken by storm by the Turks and on 30 May Muhammad II stood in the cathedral of Santa Sophia and gave thanks to the God of Islam.

The achievement of Byzantium can be expressed in a sentence. It preserved for us our classical heritage, and a movement of scholars westwards, intensified with the assault of the Turks, created the Renaissance and the civilization which has lasted from then till the twentieth century—and which seems now to be at length changing.

## JUSTINIAN

The most memorable of the emperors of Byzantium was Justinian (ruled 527–65), a man of truly Roman outlook, wide interests and somewhat staid character. It was to the amazement of his subjects that this sober ruler—

JUSTINIAN and his empress Theodora, from mosaics at Ravenna. One of the soldiers
on the left of the emperor is carrying a shield bearing the *Chi-rho* sign.

no one, they said, could remember him young—married an actress named Theodora. We see her through the eyes of an artist at Ravenna, or the historian Procopius. 'She was fair of face and charming as well, but short and inclined to pallor, not indeed completely without colour but slightly sallow. The expression of her eyes was always grim and tense.' The marriage worked. We are told that they even pretended to disagree politically so that both sides should feel that their views were understood at court. In a moment of despair it was Theodora who gave her husband courage to carry on.

Through his brilliant commander Belisarius, Justinian recovered much of the ground possessed by Rome of old. Belisarius with a remarkably small army recovered Africa from the Vandals and Italy from the Ostrogoths, and rushed to the east in time to prevent a Persian revival. But Justinian was no mere military monarch. His reign was marked, as we shall see, by important developments in law, and by sumptuous buildings including the cathedral of Santa Sophia. There was a revival of literature. One poet anticipated Ben Jonson's phrase 'Leave but a kiss within the cup.' Another wrote this moving epitaph:

> My name—my country—what are they to thee?
> What—whether base or proud my pedigree?
> Perhaps I far surpass'd all other men—
> Perhaps I fell below them all—what then?
> Suffice it, stranger! that thou seest a tomb—
> Thou know'st its use—it hides—no matter whom.

Trade with India was developed, and the Romans were able to start their own silk industry with silkworms' eggs smuggled out of China by two monks.

But all this was not achieved without cost. Justinian genuinely tried to avoid oppressive taxes, but he did not succeed.

## LAW

It is often said that Roman law is at the root of modern law. This is true; what is not always remembered is that the massive structure of Roman law as we know it, though it takes in much earlier work, belongs to the reign of Justinian and his minister of justice Tribonian. The most famous work of the reign was the *Digest*. A committee of sixteen was appointed to read and extract the two thousand books of earlier law-writers, cutting out all that was out-of-date, contradictory or repetitious. It was a colossal task; yet it was achieved in three years. By December 533 the three million lines were reduced to 150,000, in which was reared 'a holy temple of Roman justice'.

This codifying and simplifying of the law is probably the greatest single achievement of the Byzantine empire.


# ART

Byzantine art is the Bible of the illiterate. Its aim was by painting and mosaic, sometimes set on the walls or roof of churches, sometimes in images which could be held in the hand or kept in the home, to convey to the worshipper in pictures what he could not read for himself.

At one period there was a long quarrel between the Iconoclasts or Image-breakers and the Iconodules or Image-worshippers. The Iconoclasts were Puritans, religious reformers, who felt that the reverence shown to images was blasphemous; it was to worship the creation instead of the Creator. Their opponents said that they did not worship the image; rather the image helped to remind them of what they were worshipping.

From all this arise two features of Byzantine art. First, it is *stylized*. The same Bible-scenes are shown over and over again with the figures in the same position and the same attitude. It might be thought that they would be all the same, but they are not. Christ the Ruler of All may be shown in the domes of churches in the same position and attitude, but in one we may see a gentle, kindly face and in another a lean ascetic with grim blazing eyes. Secondly, Byzantine art is *unnatural*. The painting is often flat, the figures longer than in real life. This arises partly from the desire not to offend the Iconoclasts, partly because the aim is not merely to remind the worshipper of Bible-scenes but also to rouse in him feelings of awe and reverence. This explains why many people think Byzantine art crude at first, but come to enjoy it later.

The great Spanish artist whom we call The Greek, El Greco (c. 1545–1614), derived his art from Byzantium, and the revolutionary Giotto (1267–1336) has been claimed as simply a Byzantine of genius.

SOUTHERN ITALY was for a while part of the Byzantine Empire, and was permanently influenced by its art. The cathedral of Monreale in Sicily (1176) has these magnificent mosaics in the curved apse at its east end. Christ the ruler of the universe stretches his arms round the curved wall as if to embrace the worshippers in the church. Below him are his mother, angels and apostles, and below them a row of saints. Similar mosaics all round the church record scenes from the Bible.

ST SOPHIA: the cathedral of the Holy Wisdom of Christ, started in A.D. 532 in Constantinople (now Istanbul, Turkey). When the Turks captured the city in 1450, the church became a mosque. It is now a museum. The Bosporus lies behind.

The minarets belong to the mosque: to see the original effect of the cathedral, cover them.

A view of the interior.

## ST SOPHIA

The greatest achievement of Byzantine art was the cathedral of the Holy Wisdom, St Sophia, dedicated by Justinian on 27 December 537, and designed by the architect Anthemius. The nave measures 77 metres by 71·7. The crowning achievement is the dome, 55 metres up and no less than 31 across, 'a work at once marvellous and terrifying, seeming rather to hang by a golden chain from heaven than to be supported on solid masonry'. Nothing like this dome had been seen before; its weight was carried down by a series of half-domes and buttresses; it was the forerunner of the great domes of later building, St Peter's in Rome and St Paul's in London, and remains more beautiful than any.

An old poet looked at the decoration of the cathedral. 'Spring green from Carystus and Phrygian polychrome, where flowers of red and silver shine; porphyry powdered with stars; crocus glittering like gold; milk poured on a flesh of black; blue corn-flowers growing among drifts of fallen snow.' A Greek historian commented: 'On entering the church to pray, one feels at once that it was the work not of man's effort or industry, but in truth the work of the Divine Power; and the spirit, mounting to heaven, realizes that here God is very near, and that he delights in the dwelling that he has chosen for himself.' About the year 1000 six Russians visited St Sophia. 'We went to Greece, and we were led to the place where they adore their gods, and we did not know whether we were in heaven or on earth, for nowhere on earth are there such sights and such beauties.' A sober modern critic calls it 'a marvel of stability, daring, fearless logic and science'. Small wonder that Justinian cried 'Glory be to God who has counted me worthy to complete so great a work. Solomon, I have outdone you!'

## RELIGION

From all this it will be seen that the Byzantine was a religious man. Here is what one historian says of him.

His holidays were religious festivals, his performances in the circus began with the singing of hymns, his trade contracts were marked with the sign of the Cross, or contained an invocation of the Trinity, his oracles were given by hermits or through visions accorded by the holy dead, his protection lay in consecrated amulets, the most powerful remedy in his pharmacopoeia was the dust which contained a drop of sweat from the body of a stylite saint [these were holy men who hoped to please God by sitting on top of pillars for long periods, aloof from the world in prayer], his wars were crusades, his emperor the vice-gerent of God, while every startling event in nature was for him a special omen sent for his warning or encouragement.

Sometimes religion became dangerous superstition, as when the army revolted and demanded three emperors because they believed in the Trinity. In the fourth century a plague struck the city. A doctor noticed that the death-rate was higher among the poor factory-hands living in narrow basements. He said that this was due to the lack of fresh air. 'Blasphemy!' said the religious, 'a man's death is ordered by God, and air does not come into it', and when the doctor continued to visit the sufferers, caught the plague and died, they thought it a judgment on him. Yet the truth was with the doctor.

Sometimes the religion was profound, as when the emperor slept on the ground for forty nights as a penance because some of his soldiers had pillaged a church, or, returning from a victorious campaign, put a religious image in the chariot and himself walked carrying the cross.

From the religion of Byzantium sprang one of the great divisions of the Christian Church, the Holy Orthodox Catholic Apostolic Eastern Church, often called the Greek, Eastern, or Orthodox Church, which is the form Christianity takes in Russia, eastern Europe and the Near East. The Orthodox Church has great traditions, particularly in its form of worship, and has developed the idea of *fellowship* beyond that reached by the Roman Catholics with their insistence on what the pope says or the Protestants with their emphasis on the individual.


## SOCIAL LIFE

Apart from religion the social life of the empire was not very different from that of Europe today. A modern critic has pointed out how one can pick newspaper headlines from the old records. 'Prisoner of War Relief Fund Opened. Generous Responses to Appeal.' 'Wonderful Display of Shooting Stars. What does it Portend?' 'Italian's Marvellous Performing Dog.' 'Horrible Scandal in the Church. Shocking Charges Against Well-Known Bishops.' 'Audience with Abyssinian King. Weird Etiquette of an Oriental

Court.' 'White Slave Traffic in Constantinople. Royalty Intervenes.' 'Sunday Observance. New Law Passed.' 'New Baths Opened. Ingenious Heating Installation.' 'Deportation of Ballet-Dancers. Special Favour Shown to Egyptian Corps de Ballet.' 'The Jewish Massacres. Emperor's Witty Remark.' 'Earthquakes in Antioch. Terrible Damage and Loss of Life.'

One aspect of social life deserves special mention. The people were mad on horse-racing. 'If St Sophia belonged to God and the Palace to the Emperor, the hippodrome was the possession of the people.' The successful charioteer rivalled the saints in popularity. The races were interspersed with circus turns, tight-rope walkers and acrobats. But it was the races themselves which mattered; the rivalry between the Blues and the Greens and their supporters became mixed up with politics and at one time caused a serious riot. More often it turned people away from politics. They were able to let off steam harmlessly. But they took it seriously. We have discovered many buried tablets of lead inscribed with curses by which the writer hoped to 'nobble' the opposing horses.

A Byzantine noble, Theodoros Comnenos Ducas Synadenos, and his wife Eudocia Ducaena Comnena Synadena Palaeologina. The Palaeologos family was one of the ruling families, and produced several Byzantine emperors. These two formal figures in their stiff ceremonial robes, reminiscent of priestly vestments, typify Byzantine court life: elaborate, ceremonious, devout.

# THE COURT

The cathedral, the racecourse and the palace were the vital points of Byzantine culture. The palace was splendidly decorated with curious mechanical toys; lions of gold which roared and shook their tails, birds of jewellery which twittered, a throne which could be swept up to the ceiling in a moment. Such devices must have fascinated and frightened many of the primitive chiefs who came to visit the court. The emperor himself was remote and magnificent; he wore the diadem, and those admitted to his presence were expected to prostrate themselves before him. On all court occasions each member of the court had his place, his dress, his movements, his words; one of the emperors wrote them out in a book which is still preserved. The emperor was regarded as God's representative. This meant that he was far above mere humans, which made for pride, but he was also far below God, which made for humbleness.

## THE ACHIEVEMENT OF BYZANTIUM

We have already said that the achievement of Byzantium was to preserve classical culture and transmit it to the modern world. But the Byzantine empire is an interesting study in itself. W. B. Yeats, the Irish poet and mystic, in more than one poem took Byzantium as symbol of a world in which religion really mattered.

> Therefore am I come
> To the holy city of Byzantium.

# 8

# ISLAM

## ARABIA IN THE SIXTH CENTURY

THE most recent of the great world religions arose in Arabia. The town of Mecca was an important market standing on one of the major trade-routes, and a centre of religious pilgrimage for the desert peoples round about. But the religion was primitive. There was belief in spirits of all kinds, found in wells and trees and rocks, demons of the desert, goddesses of the sun and the planet Venus. We find traces of similar beliefs in Palestine in Old Testament times. The object worshipped in Mecca was a Black Stone, supposed to be of great holiness. In addition there were some Jews and Christians in the neighbourhood. It cannot have seemed a very promising setting for a religious revival.

## MUHAMMAD

The great prophet of Islam, Muhammad (c. A.D. 570–632), was slow in coming into prominence. He was brought up by an uncle, and up to the age of forty appears as a successful trader. He became business manager to a widow named Khadijah who was so impressed by his character and ability that she married him, bearing him six children. The marriage was one of deep affection, and as long as she lived Muhammad took no other wife.

At the age of forty Muhammad began to withdraw into the mountains to pray and meditate. Presently he experienced a vision of the angel Gabriel who said to him, 'You are God's messenger. Recite.' 'What shall I recite?'

> Recite in the name of your Lord who created,
> Created man from clots of blood.
> Recite. For your Lord is the most beneficent,
> Who has taught the use of the pen,
> Has taught man that which he does not know.

A copy of the Quran written for the Sultan of Morocco in 1568.

The Dome of the Rock at Jerusalem. This mosque is built above the rock from which
Muhammad traditionally ascended into heaven. The large rectangular area in which
the mosque stands is the site of the ancient temple. So this area is sacred to three
faiths: Muslim, Christian and Jewish.

Muhammad began to preach pure religion in Mecca and to denounce idolatry. He won a small band of followers, including Abu Bakr and Umar; he also met much opposition. In A.D. 622 Muhammad withdrew to the neighbouring town of Yathrib (later called Medina); this is the famous Hijrah or Hegira or Withdrawal which marks the beginning of the Muslim era. At Yathrib he was able to establish himself as a political and religious leader. There followed years of bitter struggle with Mecca in the course of which Muhammad proclaimed the duty of the *jihad* or Holy War; in 630 Mecca fell and Muhammad touched the Black Stone with his staff, calling out 'God is great' (*Allahu akbar*). He then destroyed the idols, but was generous to his opponents. Two years later he died.

## THE QURAN

The Muslims, like the Jews and Christians, are the people of a book. That book is the Quran; the name means 'that which is recited'. The Quran consists of 114 chapters or *suras*, each of which is a revelation uttered by Muhammad in a moment of inspiration. Many of the early *suras* are brief and profound. The first is used in all the daily prayers of Muslims:

*The Opening*
In the Name of God, the Compassionate, the Merciful.
    Praise be to God, Lord of the Worlds,
    The compassionate, the merciful.
    King on the Day of Judgment.
    Thee only do we worship, and to thee do we cry for help.
    Guide thou us on the straight path,
    The path of those to whom thou hast been gracious,
    With whom thou art not angry, and who go not astray.

Some of the later *suras* are longer and give detailed regulations for social life.

## THE NATURE OF GOD

*Allahu akbar. La ilaka illa 'llahu. Muhammad rasulu 'llah.* 'God is great. I testify that there is no God but Allah. I testify that Muhammad is his prophet.' These words from the call to prayer contain the essence of the

Muslim faith. Allah means the Almighty. Muhammad's vision of God is that of 'all-mightiness', of absolute power. Hence the duty of man is submission, and Islam means 'submission' and Muslim 'submissive'. The ideal believer is the *abd* or slave of God. Religion centres on revelation; it is wholly given and man's sole duty is to accept. Hence the repeated phrases: 'If Allah will', 'If Allah please', 'It shall be as Allah pleases'. It is written in the Quran 'Allah leads astray whom he pleases and guides whom he pleases, and no one knows the hosts of the Lord save himself. Every man's destiny have we fastened on his neck.'

## THE FIVE PILLARS OF FAITH

The practice of Muslim religion rests upon five 'pillars':

1. The creed or profession of faith according to the formula just quoted, pronouncing that Allah alone is God and Muhammad his Prophet.
2. Prayer five times a day, with bowed head pointing towards Mecca, preceded by a ritual washing (to make the believer clean for prayer), and accompanied by fixed gestures.
3. Fasting during the month of Ramadan, when the believer must not eat or drink during the daytime.
4. Almsgiving.
5. Pilgrimage to Mecca at least once in a lifetime.

An attempt was made to add the Holy War, especially during the military expansion of Islam; later the idea was spiritualized: 'The Holy War has ten parts, one of fighting the enemy of Islam, nine of fighting the self.'

## THE SPREAD OF ISLAM

It is possible that in the last two years of his life Muhammad was already looking beyond the boundaries of Arabia to the vision of 'One prophet, one faith for all the world'. His death was unexpected and his father-in-law Abu Bakr (ruled 632–4) took office as Caliph or Deputy. His general Khalid, a brilliant soldier nicknamed 'the Sword of God', swept into Syria and defeated the forces of Byzantium. Abu Bakr died and was succeeded by the vigorous personality of Umar (ruled 634–44). Khalid continued the conquests of Umar

The mosque at Mecca, with the Ka'aba (a shrine in which the Black Stone was set) in the centre.

A closer view of the Ka'aba surrounded by pilgrims. The building is covered with an embroidered curtain. On the right is a door through which pilgrims pass into the sanctuary.

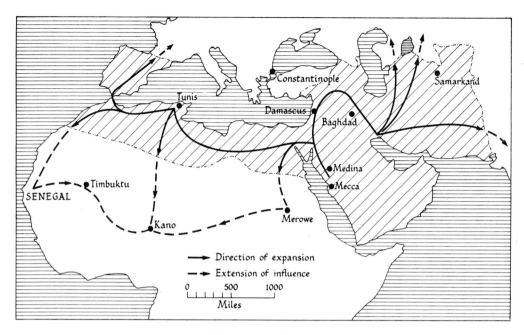

The spread of Islam.

and drove home the victory over the Byzantines. The troops stormed eastwards. Syria and Iraq fell, followed by Iran. To the west another general,
Amr, occupied Egypt and secured its corn-supply together with the great
port and mart of Alexandria. 'Islam', writes one historian, 'no longer meant
a supremacy of Medina but a common empire of the Arabs.'

There followed a period of disturbance. Arab forces pushed into Cyrenaica,
built a fortress south of Carthage and in a spectacular raid reached Tangier,
only to be compelled to withdraw again to the east. There was uncertainty
and division at home, and only under Abd-el-Malik (ruled 685–705) was the
new Umayyad dynasty firmly established, and expansion begun again. By the
end of his reign the armies of the east had reached India, and soon after there
were diplomatic relations with China. In the west the Arabs had occupied
most of North Africa by the end of the seventh century. Roman and Christian
civilization disappeared leaving cities buried in the sand and waterworks
choked in dust. In 711 the armies crossed from Morocco to Spain: the
Spaniards were divided among themselves and conquest was rapid and
thorough, leaving Spain to this day an exotic blend of Muslim and Christian

120

culture. Next they pushed through the Pyrenees into France, to be halted by Charles Martel at Poitiers in 732, just a hundred years after the prophet's death, in a battle which both sides saw as decisive in world history, for it determined whether Europe would become Muslim or remain Christian.

Shortly after, the Umayyad dynasty was succeeded by the Abbasid, and the centre of gravity moved eastwards to Persia. Here reigned the legendary Harun-al-Raschid (ruled 786–809) in absolute power and splendour; he was defender of the faith, supreme commander, chief justice, chancellor of the exchequer, and leader of worship for all true believers. But with his death the empire began to break up, though the culture remained, and the Mongol hordes of the thirteenth century only gave the death-blow to a political order already half-dead. The faith stood, and in Africa continued to spread, pushing up the Nile from Egypt and across the Sudan to Lake Chad, reaching across the Sahara along caravan routes, and at the same time expanding down the west coast from Morocco to the Senegal, inland to the ancient kingdom of Ghana (not to be confused with the modern state), across to the Niger, founding the university town of Timbuktu, and so inland again. The three streams came together at Kano, now in northern Nigeria, about 1400.

The Muslim city of Kano in Northern Nigeria. Ruled by an Emir, it is a walled city built of mud, in which the white mosque with its green dome shines all the more brightly. The buildings are arranged in walled clusters, with a little pinnacle at the corner of each.

# THE CALIPHATE

The political power of Islam lay in a strong central governor, called generally the *khalifah* or caliph—deputy or successor—sometimes the *imam* or leader (like the German *Führer* and Italian *Duce*), sometimes the commander of the faithful. The Caliph, though the religious chief of Islam, was never a pope or archbishop. His duty was to rule according to the principles laid down in the Quran, and be the political guardian of Islam. He had to be free, male, sane, commander in war and ruler in peace, and, strictly, an Arab. Islam was a monarchy, because Muslims believed in one God and one law; 'if there were more than one God, the universe would go to ruin'.

# THE SECTS

No account of Islam would be complete without mention of the sects. It is ironical that, while Muhammad condemned the Christians for splitting into sects, the faith he founded should experience the same fate.

The chief division was between the Sunnites or traditionalists and the Shi'ites or partisans. The nominal difference was over the office of Caliph, the Shi'ites holding that only the family of Ali, the prophet's nephew, had the right to succession. But the difference ran deeper. The Sunnites believed in the Quran, but also in tradition or custom, in the general agreement of scholars and in reasonable deduction from what was generally agreed. The Shi'ites rejected this and laid more stress on faith in the Leader who has disappeared and will return. This division remains today.

One sect deserves special mention. The Ismailis are a Shi'ite sect who exalt one of the eighth-century religious leaders. They believe in a series of beings between God and man—reason, soul, first matter, space and time. Reason became incarnate in a series of prophets—Adam, Noah, Abraham, Moses, Jesus, Muhammad and their own Muhammad ibn Ismail; in the end the whole creation will return to reason.

These two-and-seventy sects will remain till the Resurrection....
Love alone can end their quarrel, Love alone comes to the rescue when you cry for help
  against their arguments.
Eloquence is dumbfounded by Love.

The Court of Lions in Granada. An example of Islamic architecture in Spain.

## ART AND ARCHITECTURE

Muhammad stood against idolatry, and the Muslims discouraged representation of human beings or realistic animals, though this injunction was never strictly obeyed. The result was a wonderful flowering of what have been called the minor arts, silk and carpet, tiles and mosaic and pottery, metalwork and enamel, and exquisite ivories. The decoration of these was based sometimes on leaves and plants, sometimes on writing—Arabic script can in itself be a thing of real beauty—sometimes on abstract patterns such as geometrical shapes. The English word 'arabesque' denotes the sort of decoration the Arabs liked. 'The most casual survey of Islamic art', says one expert, 'will show that ornamental design must be ranked as the outstanding minor art evolved by Muslim genius.'

More important still is Muslim architecture. The mosque, or place of worship, is simple in its basis: a large building, with a niche showing the direction of Mecca, and a pulpit, but without statues, altars, or pews. Unusual features were the use of the Arabic script for decoration inside; the minarets or towers from which the call to prayer was issued—the oldest to survive is found near Tunis and dates from the eighth century; rather later, the use of ornamental domes of different shapes, sometimes shallow, sometimes onion-shaped; and a liking for arches of horseshoe shape, sometimes with pointed tops, sometimes rounded. The great mosque at Cordova, the blue mosque at Istanbul, the Dome of the Rock at Jerusalem, and others are among the masterpieces of the world's architecture.


## SCIENCE

Islamic scholarship usually starts from the Greeks, and from Aristotle in particular. In two fields Islamic scholars did important original work.

In mathematics they brought together knowledge from Greece and India and developed it. One example of their ability must serve. Abu-l-Wafa (940–98) calculated sine tables for intervals of 15′ *correct to 8 decimal places.* Islamic use of the numbers invented in India was so important that we still call them the Arabic numerals, and the word 'algebra' is of Arabic origin. Their greatest contribution lay in devising a symbol for zero, which made mathematics much easier.

In medicine they started from the Greeks, but added observations of their own. Al-Razi or Rhazes (*c.* 865–925) ranks as one of the greatest physicians who ever lived. His writings include essays on such subjects as 'Why people prefer quacks and charlatans to trained doctors'. His masterpiece was a treatise on smallpox and measles; his many-sidedness may be seen in his concise encyclopedia.


## LITERATURE AND THOUGHT

There are a number of Islamic writers and thinkers who ought to be better known outside Islam than they are. We may mention a few here.

Rabia (d. 801) was a woman, and at one time a slave. It was unusual for a woman to be honoured in Islam, though there was perhaps greater freedom in early days. Rabia was a mystic.

Two ways I love thee: selfishly,
Or else, as worthy is of thee.
'Tis selfish love that I do naught
Save think on thee with every thought.
'Tis purest love when thou dost raise
The veil to my adoring gaze.
In neither is the glory mine,
In both the glory must be thine.

It was Rabia who uttered the prayer: 'O my Lord, if I worship thee from fear of Hell, burn me in Hell, and if I worship thee from hope of Paradise, exclude me thence, but if I worship thee for thine own sake, then withhold not from me thine Eternal Beauty.'

Al-Farabi (d. 950) was of Turkish descent, and is reckoned by some the greatest of all Islamic thinkers. He did much to work out Greek thought in Islamic terms.

Ibn Sina, known in the West as Avicenna (980–1037), was more famous as a doctor than as a philosopher. He had an ingenious answer to the problem of how the general idea of anything (which Plato called the 'form') is related to the thing itself. It is, he said, before it in God's mind, in it in actuality, and after it in our experience. If God creates an elephant, he must first have the idea of an elephant; the idea becomes actual in the elephant created; but it is only after we have seen several elephants that we grasp the general thought of 'an elephant'.

Al-Ghazali, sometimes called Algazel (1058–1109), was nicknamed 'the Proof of Islam'. He was a sincere and profound thinker and fervent moralist. He argued that because all truth is in the Quran, there was no place for philosophical speculation.

Umar or Omar Khayyam (d. 1123) was a great mathematician who wrote an important book on algebra. He is well known in England as a poet through a felicitous rendering of his *Rubaiyat* by Edward Fitzgerald. Umar is striking for his fatalism:

The Moving Finger writes; and, having writ,
Moves on: nor all thy Piety nor Wit
  Shall lure it back to cancel half a Line,
Nor all thy Tears wash out a Word of it.

A page of the oldest surviving manuscript of Umar or Omar Khayyam's *Rubaiyat*. Umar was a Persian and, as well as being a mathematician and a poet, was an astronomer: he reformed the Persian calendar in A.D. 1079.

Bertrand Russell called him the only man to win fame as both poet and mathematician.

Ibn Rushd, known in the West as Averroes (1126–98), is by most considered the outstanding Muslim thinker, though he has had more influence in Europe than Islam. Like the others he was concerned to put Greek philosophy together with Muslim religion, and his great work was to show that they could be held together and that faith and reason did not conflict.

Jalaluddin Rumi (d. 1273) was the greatest of the Muslim mystical poets: he came from Persia.

> What is all beauty in the world? The image,
> Like quivering boughs reflected in a stream,
> Of that eternal Orchard which abides
> Unwithered in the hearts of Perfect Men.

What could be lovelier than his words 'We are the flute, our music is all Thine'?


## THE CHARACTER OF ISLAM

The great thing that Islam has given the world is its doctrine of God. There has seldom been a doctrine as majestic and awe-inspiring. God is absolute power, yet compassionate and merciful.

Alongside this is the religious fervour of Islam, a great missionary religion, eager to make converts.

Finally, the religion was worked out in life. It is just to say that the teaching of resignation (as with the Stoics) limited the scope of social reform in Islam, that there was often ruthlessness (though sometimes generosity) towards non-Muslims, and that the moral teaching of Islam seems more akin to the morals of the Old Testament than those of the New. But non-Muslims often undervalue the moral teaching of Islam. Among Muhammad's last words were these: 'People! Listen to my words and be sure you understand. Every Muslim is the brother of every other Muslim. All of you are of the same equality.' One historian remarked that Muhammad spread through the Middle East 'a broader, cleaner, fresher, more vigorous political and social ideal than that of the decadent Byzantine Empire'.

# 9

# THE MIDDLE AGES

## THE BARBARIAN KINGDOMS

A MAP of the Roman empire provides a sad commentary on our modern divisions; its massive unity stands as a silent rebuke. But lying across the line of the Danube and the Rhine were an ill-assorted throng of miscellaneous tribes bearing names which were later to become familiar in European geography: across the Rhine were the Frisians, Franks and Alemanni; across the Danube the Visigoths; and in the unexplored expanse of central Europe, stretching across the Vistula into Russia, lay Angles and Saxons, Lombards and Burgundians, Vandals, Ostrogoths and Huns. The key to the situation probably lay with the Huns. They are familiar in Chinese history and seem to have formed a buffer through whom movements on the west frontiers of China spread across to Europe. At any rate, something set the peoples of Central Europe, and particularly the Goths from the Baltic, on the move. The Roman empire, weakened by plague and other disrupting forces, could no longer withstand them. The sea-wall broke; the waves surged in, and, as we have seen, Rome itself fell to Alaric in A.D. 410 and a shudder echoed round the world. By 500 the Vandals were in North Africa, the Visigoths in Spain and the south of France (though not in the region of Portugal, which then as now was independent), the Ostrogoths held Italy and Yugoslavia, the Burgundians were established round Lyons, and the Franks were already in the northern part of that country to which they were to give their name.

## THE BEGINNINGS OF THE FEUDAL SYSTEM

Tribal organization was often simple. There was a leader, outstanding in prowess, or sometimes in counsel, to whom his followers owed allegiance.

128

When the tribe broke victoriously through to an area in which they could settle, the leader would endow his lieutenants with land on condition that they offered him continued service when he called upon them. They became his vassals; he became their *seigneur* or lord. Already in the Frankish domain of the seventh century was to be seen a society based on status, starting with the overlord, through the subsidiary landowners, down to the peasants and finally the slaves. In this society the weak owed service to the strong but the strong also had a duty to protect the weak. There was a two-way obligation. The system, which is generally called feudalism, spread rapidly in the tenth and eleventh centuries, and became the normal structure of society in the Middle Ages.

Alongside this vigorous leader-follower relationship were the germs of democracy in the form of tribal assemblies. These in themselves were lost as the tribes became settled, but the idea of individual responsibility remained, especially in local courts of justice.


## THE CHURCH

From the first expansion the Christian Church had looked to Rome as the centre of the civilized world. Suetonius tells us that in A.D. 53 the Jews were expelled from the capital for creating a disturbance on the instigation of one Chrestus; it looks as if his story is garbled and there was in fact the sort of trouble between Jews and Christians we read of in the book of Acts. Paul yearned to go there, and Peter followed him to a common martyrdom. The traditions of the Church in Rome thus extended back to the leader of the apostles, and that combined with the prestige attaching to the city itself to make the bishop of Rome the most powerful authority in the church as a whole, though his position was challenged by Constantinople, Jerusalem and Alexandria at different times. The title of Pope (*Papa* means Father), which was at first applied to other bishops, became peculiarly his. His power was huge; the pagan Praetextatus used to remark jokingly to Pope Damasus: 'Make me bishop of the Church of Rome, and I will become a Christian without more ado.' When Rome fell, the prestige which had belonged to the state became attached to the Church, and across the centuries the very fact that under the feudal system the commons had no freedom in western Europe made for the expansion of the Church to fulfil the needs of the people.

No individual did more for the authority of the church than Gregory I, rightly called the Great, who was pope from 590 to 604. A Roman noble by birth, in his youth he held high political office. But his piety outstripped his ambition. He gave up worldly prizes to become a monk, and it was against his will that he was called to that high place in the Church which his abilities demanded. His chief historical importance lies in his claim for the absolute primacy of the bishopric of Rome: 'I know of no bishop who is not subject to the Apostolic See, when a fault has been committed.' This claim, though it may have been implicit before, had hardly been made so explicitly. He has other claims on our attention. He encouraged missions. A famous story told how in his younger days he saw some attractive strangers in the slave-market. Being told that they were Angles, he exclaimed, 'Not Angles but angels'. He never forgot them, and when he became pope, in 597, sent a monk who bore the same name as the great theologian Augustine to bring Christianity to the island of Britain, which the Romans had abandoned two centuries before. So the preacher penetrated where the sword failed, and Canterbury, where Augustine settled, became the centre of British Christianity. Gregory encouraged the monks. He was a noble pastor to his clergy.

He was devoted to his task, filled with belief in the rights and duties of his office, stern to himself and others, dominating others, tireless in sickness and health, spurred by a passionate sense of justice and an active benevolence....To the Papacy he gave a practical programme in action which was to inspire and outlast the Middle Ages. In a barbarizing world he maintained higher standards and ideals, and preserved them by his deeds and writing for posterity.


## CHARLEMAGNE AND THE HOLY ROMAN EMPIRE

By the middle of the seventh century the Merovingian dynasty, which ruled over the Franks, had become weak and ineffective. But weakness on the throne encouraged strength in those immediately below the throne. A succession of strong men held the post of mayors of the palace, and eventually ousted the old dynasty, being known as the Carolingians. Pepin II (mayor 680–714) established Frankish supremacy across the Rhine, where he encouraged Christian missions. Charles Martel—the nickname means 'Hammer'—(mayor 719–41) was one of the most successful military com-

The throne of Charlemagne in the cathedral at Aachen, the capital of his original empire. On Christmas Day, 800, the Holy Roman Empire was established at his coronation. On his throne successive emperors were crowned king, until the sixteenth century. They then went to Rome to receive the Imperial Crown from the Pope.

manders of all time; as we have seen, he checked the Muslim armies at Poitiers in 732 and further extended the power of the Franks in Germany. His sons Pepin the Short (mayor 741–51; king 751–68) and Carloman (joint mayor 741–7) were brought up in a monastery. Pepin is a man undervalued by history. With him the title of power was added to the possession of power, and the new dynasty, which took its name from his father, began. More important, with him came the idea that political authority was a Christian responsibility. 'To us the Lord has entrusted the care of government.' He used his authority to strengthen the Church, and to enforce, for instance, tithes, Sunday as a day of rest, and the Christian concept of marriage. 'Though at the present our power is not enough for everything,' he said, 'if God gives us peace and leisure later, we hope to restore fully the standards of the saints.'

His son Charles the Great, Charlemagne, ruled from 768 to 814. He extended his dominion far into Germany and Central Europe, south-west into Spain, where he was repulsed in a retreat which became legendary, south-east to the occupation of North Italy; it was too large to be administered by anyone lacking his dynamic energy, and after his death it began to fall apart. He brought in wild tribes which he was not able to unite in any real sense with the Franks. His own court was cultured, with the English scholar Alcuin (d. 804) to give a lead. Above all, though Charles was implacably ambitious, with one of those curious contradictions to which human beings are prone, we cannot doubt that he was also sincerely Christian. It seems that he had not planned the action of the pope when on Christmas Day 800 the latter approached the king as he knelt in prayer and laid a golden crown on his head, while the people cried 'God grant life and victory to Charles, Augustus, crowned by God, great peace-maker and Emperor of the Romans'. Byzantium had ceased to count in the West, and Charles accepted the calling with all that it implied. He was the new David, God's anointed. There were in his mind two powers, the priestly and the imperial, given by God to rule men, and though the priest had placed the crown on the emperor's head, Charles also knew that the Church was under his care, and regarded himself as the defender of Christendom and head of the Church. He went back across the Alps, and his subjects reasserted their vow to him as emperor, each being warned

that his vow of homage was not merely a promise to be true to the emperor and to serve him against his enemies, but a promise to live in obedience to God and his law according to the best of each man's strength and understanding. It was a vow to abstain from theft and oppression and injustice, no less than from heathen practices and witchcraft: a vow to do no wrong to the churches of God, nor to injure widows and orphans, of whom the emperor is the chosen protector and guardian.

So was born the idea of the Holy Roman Empire, an idea of immeasurable importance which ushered in the Middle Ages, and remained the centre of their political thought, and which tottered to its fall only in the nineteenth century, when it had long ceased to be either holy or Roman. Here in a

The imperial crown of the Holy Roman Empire, probably made for the imperial coronation of Otto the Great in Rome in 962. In shape the crown is said to be a reminiscence of the Roman laurel wreath (the circle of the crown itself) and the Roman helmet (the crown has an arch, concealed behind the cross, which would be something like the crest of a helmet; and it also had hanging ear-pieces, now removed). The circlet has eight facets: eight was a number associated with the idea of perfection.

The Holy Roman Empire was meant to be a Christianized revival of the old Roman empire. Christ was its head, and the emperor his deputy. The crown was placed on the emperor's head by Christ's other representative, the pope, head of the universal Church. In the Middle Ages the empire became a political body sometimes in conflict with the pope. Though it always retained some prestige, it tended to dwindle until it was no more than the unifying bond between the German-speaking states. It was finally dissolved in 1806, as the victorious Napoleon approached Vienna.

visible political institution, Church and state were one, and the unity of Christendom expressed. The emperor was one embodiment of this, the pope another; the relation between them remained to be worked out.

## HILDEBRAND

For two-and-a-half centuries the relation was an uneasy compromise. Then came a pope who was not afraid to stand firm. In 1073 Archdeacon Hildebrand took office as Gregory VII and laid down his position in no uncertain terms: 'Come now, I pray you, O most holy Fathers and Princes' (he means Peter and Paul), 'that all the world may know that if you are able to bind and loose in heaven you are able on earth to take away, or to give to each, according to his merits, empires, kingdoms, duchies, marquisates, counties, and the possessions of all men.' The meaning is clear; the Church is lord of the state. Accordingly when King Henry IV of Germany, later Holy Roman Emperor, defied him, he issued a sentence of excommunication, and Henry, finding his power crumbling away, had to cross the Alps in the depths of winter to the castle at Canossa, and stand, a barefoot penitent, three days in the snow before the pope would deign to absolve him. Hildebrand was a tireless reformer within the Church, who fought against simony, the winning of high office in the Church by bribery. In the end his enemies were too strong for him and he had to leave Rome. He died on 25 May 1085, with the words—a bitter misquotation from the 45th psalm—'I have loved righteousness and hated iniquity; therefore I die in exile.' His assertion of papal power remained. In the twelfth century a Byzantine ambassador remarked 'Your pope is not a bishop but an emperor'; in the thirteenth the pope could say to an imperial delegation: 'Is it not mine to guard the laws of the Empire? I, I am the Emperor.'

## THE CRUSADES

The crusades must be reckoned one of the most tragically futile episodes in human history. The work of Hildebrand was soon taken up by Pope Urban II. He picked up an idea which his great predecessor had sketched, a crusade to recover the holy places of Palestine for Christendom. As Isocrates,

134

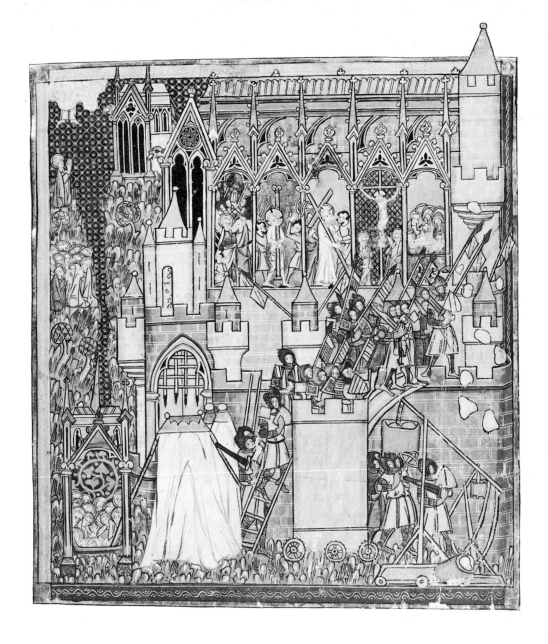

The Capture of Jerusalem by the crusaders, on 15 July 1099.
  The besieging crusaders leave their tents and scale the city walls, while others hurl
huge stones from machines.  Note, to the left and above, the scenes from the life of
Christ, which emphasize that in taking Jerusalem the crusaders were winning the holy
places of their faith.

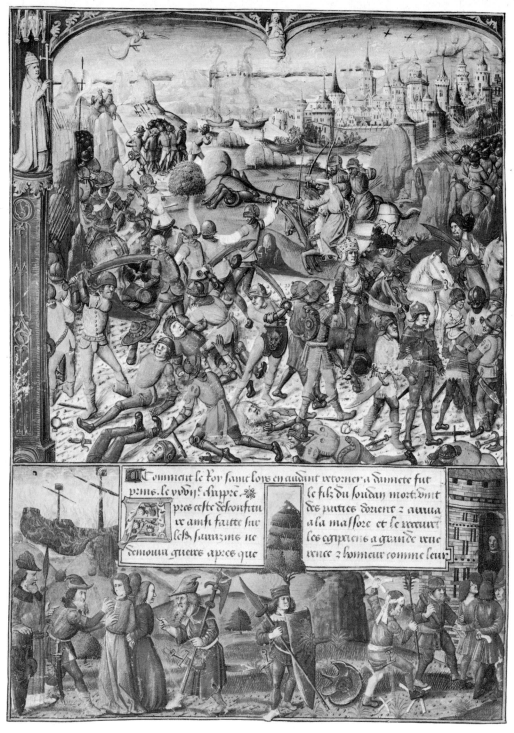

The defeat of the crusaders, and the capture of King Louis IX of France, at Mansura in Egypt in April 1250. So many crusaders were captured that they were an embarrassment to the victorious Egyptians, and were slaughtered at the rate of 300 per day for a week.

This was one of the most humiliating defeats suffered by the crusaders in their 200-year-long struggle to maintain a Christian empire in the heart of the Muslim world. When at last they were defeated, after four major crusades, and innumerable wars, battles and atrocities on both sides, the way was clear for the Muslim conquest of Byzantium, and the advance to the very gates of Vienna in the sixteenth century.

centuries before, had tried to end the struggle of Greek with Greek in a common war against the Persian, so Urban tried to end the struggle of Christian with Christian in a common war against the Muslim. In a great speech at Clermont in 1095 he outlined his plan. The common symbol of the crusaders should be the cross; their battle-cry 'Deus volt', 'It is the will of God'. The assembly ended in tumultuous, surging cries of 'Deus volt' and a rush for crosses. Urban sent a publicist of genius, Peter the Hermit, to recruit for his campaign; he reinforced his challenge with the promise of forgiveness of sins to those who volunteered and eternal blessedness to those who fell. The result was an immense rise in the prestige and power of the pope.

It is not needful to go into the sorry details of all that followed. The crusaders quarrelled among themselves; they were inefficient and ill-led; they were sometimes brutally cruel to those through whose lands they passed; one leader massacred all the Jews he could lay his hands on, the beginning of the blackest stain on the Middle Ages; many were diverted from their professed object by chances of enriching themselves. Yet all was not loss. The nations of Europe had shown a unity they had lost for centuries and have never yet recaptured. The enthusiasm was often noble and sacrificial; it was tragic that it could not be given in a more constructive cause at the time, but as the centuries passed the crusading spirit did not wholly perish and men came to crusade against social wrongs, such as slavery and child-labour, by peaceful means. Further, the crusades enlarged the vision of western Europe, which had become narrowed and darkened, and brought back contact with Greek thought in a way that created the learned culture of the Middle Ages, as renewed contact three centuries later was to produce the Renaissance.

## FRANCIS AND DOMINIC

The early thirteenth century saw a revival of Christian devotion. Francis of Assisi (c. 1181–1226) was a light-hearted man-about-town of romantic ideals. One day, faced with a sufferer from leprosy, a disease which he had always loathed, he made a sudden resolve to kiss the man's sores. From then he was a changed person. Care for the suffering became central to his life, and he gave up all his privileges. He took to himself the words with which Jesus

The twelfth-century (Romanesque) bell-tower of Assisi cathedral, and the castle of Rocca Maggiori overlooking the town. The cathedral was standing in the time of St Francis; the castle was built later.

had sent out his immediate followers, and himself, as he said, took as his mistress 'My Lady Poverty' and went out with no possessions to preach the gospel of repentance 'with words which were like fire, penetrating the heart'. Others had done the same. What distinguished Francis was his rare combination of gaiety and sympathy. 'More than a saint among saints, among sinners he was as one of themselves.' His understanding extended to birds and animals, who loved him; to this day real doves nest in the arms of his statue at Assisi. He was at one with all nature, and could welcome death as his brother in God's creation. His mighty hymn of praise is still sung in many forms. Others followed him; so was formed the order of Friars Minor or

St Francis preaching to the birds.
From the fresco by Giotto at Assisi.

Grey Friars as they were called, living on alms and odd jobs, reaching out with healing words and good works, bringing religion into the ordinary life of ordinary people.

About the same time Dominic (1170–1221) founded the order of Friars Preacher or Black Friars. Less revolutionary and magnetic in person than Francis, he was a superb organizer and sought, with success, to bring together a group of dedicated scholars who, living in simplicity, would study the Christian faith and defend it against all comers.

Thus popular preaching and scholarly study were invoked in defence of Christianity, both thoroughly constructive measures. It was unfortunate that at the same time the Church should have felt the need to massacre dissenters in the south of France and to establish the tribunals of the Inquisition which, however sincere, used torture to make people confess, and imposed such punishments as public flogging in church, solitary confinement for life, and, if all else failed, burning at the stake.

The great founders of the medieval religious orders standing, St Benedict, St Bernard, St Romuald, kneeling, St Francis (bearing the stigmata, the wounds of Christ), St John of Malta, St Thomas Aquinas, Peter of Verona the martyr. Fresco by Fra Angelico in St Mark's, Florence.

# LYRIC POETRY

As literacy declined under the barbarian invasions, the artificial patterns of classical poetry, based on *quantity* (the length of time it takes to pronounce a syllable, like the minims and crotchets of modern music) rather than *accent* or *stress* (like the accent on the first beat of a bar in music) fell away. Poetry was increasingly spoken or sung rather than written, and began to conform to the rhythms of natural speech. The result was a gain in freshness, and a heritage of charming lyric, often anonymous. Sometimes this was composed in the service of the Church, as in the tremendous:

> Dies irae, dies illa
> solvet saeclum in favilla
> teste David cum Sibylla.

Sometimes the poem was a poem of love:

> She stood in her scarlet gown,
>    If anyone touched her,
>    The gown rustled.    Eia!

> She stood in her scarlet gown,
>    Her face like a rose,
>    And her mouth like a flower.    Eia!

Other songs were songs of drink; the Archpoet claimed his wages with the words 'The quality of my verses depends on the wine.'


# THE MEDIEVAL MANUSCRIPT

The monasteries preserved the great works of the past. One of the results of this work has been the preservation of illustrated or illuminated manuscripts, decked with exquisite miniature painting. It is possible to trace these illustrations back to the art of classical times, for the monks often went to classical art when they wanted to depict Christian scenes, and a miniature of Christ may have its origin in Heracles or Orpheus. Among such illuminated manuscripts we may instance the French calendars, with scenes showing the labour of the several months, and the Irish Book of Kells, in which individual letters are drawn with all the resources of Celtic ornament.

A page from a fifteenth-century French illuminated manuscript of Froissart's chronicles. The illumination shows the entry of the child King Louis II of Anjou into Paris, which is shown as a typical medieval city with a fortified wall and the spires of many churches. Notice the head-dresses of the royal ladies and their fashionable shaved foreheads. The text is written in pointed French script, and the whole page surrounded by a border of flowers and fruit. Such a manuscript would be written and decorated to the special order of a wealthy, and perhaps noble, purchaser.

# GOTHIC ARCHITECTURE

The most enduring legacy of the Middle Ages is its architecture. Its castles are mostly impressive ruins; its cathedrals stand. Four distinctive styles followed one another at intervals of approximately a century. The years 1050–1150 mark the high point of the style which in England is called Norman and on the continent of Europe Romanesque. This style is marked by solidity of construction, and by rounded arches, embellished with zig-zag or similar ornaments. Winchester in England and Hildesheim in Germany show its chief features. Its greatest glory, however, is Durham cathedral, with its unrivalled setting above the river Wear; here the sense of solid permanence is found, but also a new lightness, created by the ribbed vaulting which was to be a major feature of the Gothic style.

The years 1150–1250 saw the beginnings of Gothic architecture proper. In Britain the style is denoted Early English. The ribbed vaulting of Durham came into general use. Equally important was the pointed arch. With round arches it is possible to vault a square only, or the arches will be of different heights. A pointed arch makes possible much greater variety. Further, buttresses, sometimes 'flying buttresses' (free shafts of stone carrying the thrust from an inner to an outer wall), replaced the massive walls of the older cathedrals and lightened the appearance of the whole. At St Denis in France the new style first appears; the purest example in England is Salisbury. The great French cathedrals of Paris, Chartres, Amiens and Rheims belong to these years, though they are in some ways more akin to the English cathedrals which followed them. Chartres in particular is one of the wonders of the world with the glorious blue of its stained glass and the carved figures of the western front adding to its other beauties. This climax to cathedral-building on the Continent is called High Gothic.

The years 1250–1350 saw a style in England often called Decorated, with flowing geometrical tracery and a rich outpouring of inventive patterns. Bristol and Ely offer good examples of the period. But the period is essentially transitional; it is a working out of what has gone before. More important is the revolutionary change to Perpendicular. Again we may date this approximately 1350–1450, though of the two finest examples, one, Gloucester cathedral, is rather earlier and the other, King's College chapel, Cambridge, rather later. Arches were flattened, walls became screens of glass with slim vertical lines of stone, vaulting was complex and ornamental. In eastern England prosperity in the wool-trade led to small 'cathedrals' being built in the villages. Here the wood-carvers came into their own, and anyone visiting Norfolk is well-advised to see the wonderful roof at Knapton, which Dorothy Sayers used as a feature in her detective-story *The Nine Tailors*.

These buildings tell us a lot about the Middle Ages. The skill of craftsmen was given to the service of God, and for long given anonymously. The centre of life, whether in town or village, was the worship of God, and these mighty buildings remain a reminder of that fact. Few, except incurable romantics, would wish to have lived in the Middle Ages. But it is undeniable that it was a time in which religion was taken seriously.

The Benedictine abbey church of Maria Laach in the Rhineland, Germany, was built between 1093 and 1156. Note the smallness of the windows, which leaves the massive walls comparatively unbroken.

Romanesque architecture is earlier than Gothic, which grew out of Romanesque, though the two can often be found combined in one building. The characteristics of Romanesque are massiveness and simplicity; the most important single feature is the round arch.

The diagram shows the great abbey church of Cluny in Burgundy, France, begun in 1089, and destroyed after the French Revolution. A basically simple plan, somewhat similar to that of Maria Laach, has become complicated by the multiplication of each of its parts, especially all the little semicircular chapels clustered round the east end (on the right). Cluny was an immensely important monastic centre, with many daughter abbeys in other countries. It was therefore a source of architectural influence.

This diagram is taken from Meister Erwin von Steinbach's sketch of 1275 for the west front of the Minster at Strassburg. Three doorways were to be surmounted by a round rose-window and two immensely tall delicate spires (almost 400 feet high). The whole effect is of soaring upward movement.

The west front of Amiens cathedral (1225–30) shows the source of some of the features of Meister Erwin's design. France was the fountainhead of Gothic. Note the line of statues below the rose-window, and the shadows of the 'flying buttresses' at the extreme left.

Gothic church architecture gives an immedia[te] impression of height, with its great spir[es] pointing to heaven like a constant reminder [of] God's presence. The pointed arch takes t[he] place of the rounded windows and vaults [of] Romanesque. In effect this meant muc[h] greater engineering skill; the weight of t[he] great towers, spires, and vaulted roofs w[as] borne at certain points of stress by pillar[s,] arches and buttresses. Therefore the wa[lls] could be almost removed, and more elabora[te] windows inserted (see Cologne cathedr[al] below).

Inside Cologne cathedral, Germany: a long narrow uninterrupted nave, with the slender columns springing up and joining, in the vaulted roof, like a row of immensely tall slim trees. The wall of the choir at the east end beyond the altar is almost entirely glass from floor to roof.

The crossing of the nave and transepts (1338) at Wells cathedral in England shows a supreme example of the beauty of Gothic engineering. The enormous weight of the central tower is taken by intersecting arches which might have been designed for the mere sake of their beauty of line.

England developed its own Gothic styles. Salisbury cathedral was built between 1220 and 1266: the graceful central tower was begun in 1334. Note the 'flying buttresses' springing from the side of the central nave. The long wall leading to the right shuts off the cloisters: a reminder that cathedrals were usually associated with monasteries.

Medieval architects were as much concerned with castles as with churches. Conway castle in Wales is an example of a typical British medieval fortification; and a reminder of the extent to which in frontier areas it was important for the inhabitants to be able to withdraw into the safety of strong stone walls. Castles were usually situated on high ground; and if possible with water on at least one side, to make them more difficult to attack.

# THE UNIVERSITIES

The other lasting monument of the Middle Ages is the university. The early universities were at first called *studia generalia* or places of study to which all might come. The first was at Salerno in Italy, where Medicine was the chief subject of study. This was followed by Bologna, where Law was the speciality. Bologna is of particular interest because it was for some years managed by the students, who appointed and paid their lecturers, and fined them if they were late. The most important university of the north was at Paris. The cathedral school had enjoyed the presence of the great scholar Peter Abelard (1079–1142), whose tragic love-affair has made him a favourite theme for poets and novelists. The university which followed was a guild of scholars with their apprentices, who would, when qualified, be accepted as 'masters' just as an apprentice to a trade aspired to be a master-craftsman. The universities of Oxford and Cambridge belong to the same period of the twelfth or early thirteenth century. The universities were a new factor in the situation, and the scholar came to take his place alongside priest and monarch; Church, state and university were now the three powers given by God to guide the world.

## THOMAS AQUINAS AND THE SCHOOLMEN

In the cathedral schools had been found the intellectual defenders of the faith. Anselm (1033–1109) stands as the greatest scholar in the line of archbishops of Canterbury; he attempted to prove the existence of God by pure logic. At Paris Abelard was the outstanding figure. But the principal constructive thinker of the Middle Ages was Thomas of Aquino (1225–74), sometimes called the Angelic Doctor. Thomas was a Dominican; the freedom of the new universities had led to the admission of all sorts of opinions; Thomas set himself to defend the Christian faith by reason. He is sometimes today regarded as a conservative thinker; in his own time he was a revolutionary in bringing the thought of Aristotle into a massive whole with the Christian faith. He sought to demonstrate the existence of God by five arguments:

1. All motion must have a beginning. God is the beginning of motion.
2. The world is made up of a chain of causes and effects. God is the first cause.

3. Nothing we see about us *must* exist. But there must be some being which *must* exist, or nothing would exist. That being is God.

4. There must be a highest point in the ladder of perfection; that point is God.

5. The world shows purpose and design; this implies a designer, God.

Starting from these foundations Thomas built a tremendous system which has lasted as the intellectual structure of the Catholic Church.

## DANTE

In some ways the most characteristic figure of the Middle Ages is Dante (1265–1321). Poet, philosopher, theologian, politician—he was so acknowledged in his lifetime—he stands before us as the man of integrated life; his field was the world, under God. His home was Florence; he shared in its politics, and cared enough for its peace to send one of his own friends, Guido Cavalcanti, into exile. Not long after, the pendulum swung, and he was himself exiled. He never came back; when offered return on terms he could not accept he replied: 'Can I not everywhere behold the light of the sun and the stars; everywhere meditate on the noblest truths, without appearing ingloriously before the city and the people?' He came to a new breadth of vision—'My country is the whole world'—and a new depth of political thought, expressed in his Latin work *On Kingship*, where 'his ideal emperor is a just and humane judge, dependent on God only, the heir of the universal sway of Rome, to which belonged the sanction of nature, of right and of the will of God'. He hoped for a single state throughout the world, and that emperor and pope would work side by side to give human beings prosperity in this world and bliss in the next.

As a young man he had fallen in love with a lady named Beatrice, and there must be few who will not thrill to the story of that love as he relates it, and Dante Gabriel Rossetti translates it, in *The New Life*.

> My lady looks so gentle and so pure
> When yielding salutation by the way,
> That the tongue trembles and has naught to say,
> And the eyes, which fain would see, may not endure.
> And still, amid the praise she hears secure,
> She walks with humbleness for her array;

DANTE, a detail from Raphael's great group-composition on the subject of the church on earth and in Heaven. The poet's characteristic features are clearly represented: the laurel-wreath is the symbol of his poetic inspiration. It became the custom in Renaissance times for cities and academies to award the laurel-wreath ceremonially to famous poets (a revival of the classical Roman custom). The award to Dante was significant because he wrote in his native Italian, not in Latin.

Seeming a creature sent from Heaven to stay
On earth, and show a miracle made sure.
She is so pleasant in the eyes of men
That through the sight the inmost heart doth gain
A sweetness which needs proof to know it by:
And from between her lips there seems to move
A soothing essence that is full of love,
Saying for ever to the spirit, 'Sigh!'

But already the love of woman is pointing him to something higher; Beatrice refusing him her salutation becomes a symbol and a warning. In exile he at first seemed to lose his vision. In *The Banquet* his old love is challenged by a new, My Lady Philosophy. Then he recovered himself, and in his greatest work *The Divine Comedy* the imagined figure of Beatrice unites his two former loves. In his vision the poet visits Hell, Purgatory and Paradise; the whole shows a wonderful understanding of human nature. Dante, like Thomas, links Christianity and Aristotle; his final word is that there is one principle which both makes the world go round and leads man to salvation, 'Love, which rules the sun and the other stars'. The poem was written in Italian; in the use of his native tongue rather than Latin, and in his many-sidedness Dante looks forward to the Renaissance. But in the unity of a vision which centres upon God, not man, he is wholly of the Middle Ages.


## THE MIDDLE AGES

As we look back at the Middle Ages in Europe we see a world in which religion was central to life, in which there was an attempt to make religion and politics walk hand in hand, an attempt to apply belief in life, in which there was at least in theory one Church and one emperor; defects are obvious. The structure of society gave protection (of a sort) but no freedom to the lower classes; scientific advances were few and disease prevalent; the standard of living was generally low; there was much cruelty, much weakness, much hypocrisy. But the relevance of religion and the unity of thought were great things, and the universities, cathedrals and the writings of Thomas and Dante remain to remind us of them.

# THE RENAISSANCE AND REFORMATION

## THE BREAK-UP OF THE MIDDLE AGES

BY the end of the fourteenth century the massive unity of the medieval world was creaking at the joints. For the change which took place in the fifteenth and sixteenth centuries we can trace three broad reasons.

The first is economic. The theory on which the Middle Ages stood has been well analysed by R. H. Tawney:

Society, like the human body, is an organism composed of different members. Each member has its own function: prayer, or defence, or merchandise, or tilling the soil. Each must receive the means suited to its station, and must claim no more. Within classes there must be equality; if one takes into his hand the living of two, his neighbour will go short. Between classes there must be inequality; for otherwise a class cannot perform its function, or—a strange thought to us—enjoy its rights. Peasants must not encroach on those above them. Lords must not despoil peasants. Craftsmen and merchants must receive what will maintain them in their calling, and no more.

Combined with this was the view that the world of economics was subject to moral law; in particular usury, the lending of money on condition of receiving extra money on repayment, was regarded as a sin; so was avarice, or the desire for gain itself. This was the theory, but Benvenuto de Imola remarked bitterly: 'If a man takes usury he goes to hell; if he doesn't, he goes to the poorhouse.' There was in fact quite a lot of expansive money-making in the Middle Ages, and the expansion began to burst the seams of medieval theory and medieval geography. For the medieval world was a closed world, except for trade with the east (developed by Venice). When this was cut off by the rise of Turkey under the Osmanli dynasty, changes were bound to come.

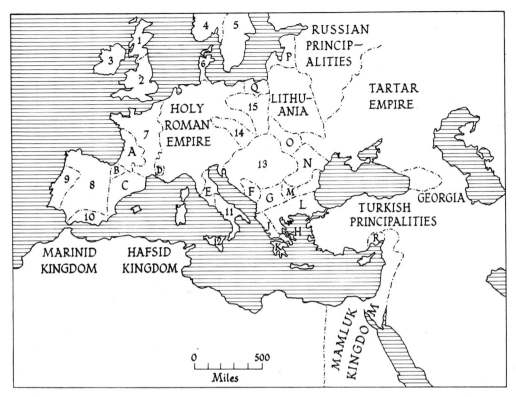

States and Kingdoms in the later Middle Ages

| STATES | | KINGDOMS | |
|---|---|---|---|
| A Guienne | K Achaia | 1 Scotland | 8 Castile |
| B Navarre | L Byzantium | 2 England | 9 Portugal |
| C Aragon | M Bulgaria | 3 Ireland | 10 Granada |
| D Avignon | N Moldavia | 4 Norway | 11 Naples |
| E Papal State | O Galicia | 5 Sweden | 12 Sicily |
| F Bosnia | P Estonia | 6 Denmark | 13 Hungary |
| G Serbia | Q Prussia | 7 France | 14 Bohemia |
| H Athens | R Armenia | | |
| J Epirus | | | |

Secondly, as we have seen, the pressure of the Turks upon the senile Byzantine empire led to a movement of scholars westward. It used to be thought that this movement dated from the fall of Constantinople in 1453. We see now that it was more gradual. Thus in the years 1397–1400 a Byzantine scholar named Manuel Chrysoloras was lecturing in Florence, and in 1438–9 the distinguished philosopher Georgius Gemistus Plethon (c. 1355–1450), on

155

a visit to the same city, did much to replace the influence of Aristotle by that of Plato. The first renewed contact with Greek culture helped to create the thought-world of the Middle Ages; we have seen it in Thomas Aquinas and Dante. The second created the thought-world of the Renaissance.

Thirdly, the authority of the Church was undermined by the corruption within it. The Church—inevitably in the situation—was the biggest business in the world, and—though this should not have been inevitable—fell into the ways of the world. Money-lenders whom Dante thought fit for hell were given by the pope the title of 'peculiar sons of the Roman Church'. Usury was found within the Church itself; so was simony. The riches of the Church contrasted ill with the suffering of the poor. Even the glories of cathedral architecture have to be seen against this background. 'The Church is resplendent in her walls, beggarly in her poor. She clothes her stones in gold and leaves her sons naked.' The break-up of the Church came over the sale of indulgences. Men were expected to pay for documents which professed to grant forgiveness of any sin they might commit. This was bad enough, but it was only part of a deeper corruption.

## CAPITALISM

Already by the end of the Middle Ages something which we might call capitalism had appeared in Flanders and Florence; that is to say that industry and a system of finance were being organized by the rich owners in order that they might become more rich. This system, with all that it implied, had by the seventeenth century largely replaced the stable order of the Middle Ages. What it meant was, first, that industry and commerce came to a new importance, and farming fell away and began to get into difficulties. Secondly, a society based on *contract* began to replace a society based on *status*. In the old order the landowner and the peasant working on the land each had his God-given position, his rights and responsibilities. In the new order the worker came to a bargain with the capitalist and sold his labour for wages; the responsibility began and ended with the terms of that bargain. Thirdly, money mattered more than birth or position, and a new class, the middle class, arose with a power which depended on money, alongside the vassals of the kings and the nobles in their courts. Fourthly, the moral judgment of

The town hall of Bruges in Belgium, with its 297-foot-high belfry, is a symbol of the growing influence and wealth of the merchants in the late Middle Ages. The building was completed in the fourteenth century, the belfry in 1482.

economics was dropped. People no longer asked the question 'Is it right?', but instead 'Does it work?', not 'What is the just price?' but 'What is the least he will take?' or 'What is the most he will pay?'. Fifthly, as a result of this, the old idea of service (preached even when it was not practised) was replaced by self-seeking, and the old idea of the community by an emphasis on the individual. The new order was 'Each for himself, and the devil take the hindmost'. The result was an increase in prosperity for the successful and in suffering for the unsuccessful.

157

Within the illustration:

Ti commence li liures du graunt Caaii qui parole de la graunt Ermeiue de perse
et desarrans et dinde. Et des grauz merueille qui p̃ le moude sont.

Our savoir la pure verite des ⬧ bles sauz nule mencouge. Et chascus qui cr liure oiia

VENICE, a great city-republic founded on exploration, trade, and banking. An illumination in a fifteenth-century French manuscript. Notice the shop on the left, the street vendor, the water carrier and the groups of elegantly dressed citizens. The great cathedral of St Mark is in the top left corner. The shore at the bottom is inhabited by lions and other wild beasts; so you are to imagine a vast ocean between the top and bottom of the picture.

# EXPLORATION

The search for wealth led to a search for new markets. The new contact with the Greeks led to a new spirit of inquiry. Already in the thirteenth century the Polos, Venetian merchants, had pioneered far into Asia, where they reached the lordly pleasure-dome of Kublai Khan at Xanadu. It is significant that Prince Henry the Navigator was inspired by the account of their travels, and that when printing was invented in the fifteenth century *The Travels of Marco Polo* was one of the first books to be printed. Henry (1394–1460) was a prince of Portugal; his captains reached Madeira (where he left a colony to grow sugar) and the Azores, and explored the west coast of Africa as far as the Senegal and the Gambia. Advance was now swift. In 1482–3 Diego Cam discovered the Congo. In 1487 Bartholomew Diaz reached a cape in the far south of Africa. He called it 'Cape of Storms', but the king renamed it 'Cape of Good Hope'. In the same year Covilhan sailed from the Red Sea to India and made a thorough exploration of those waters. In 1497–8 Vasco da Gama opened up the sea-route to India via the Cape of Good Hope, and by 1520 Portuguese contact was firmly made with China. Meantime other nations were not idle. The Spaniards through Christopher Columbus and Amerigo Vespucci (from whom America takes its name) had reached the West Indies and explored central and south America, and in 1519–22 Magellan, a former page at the Portuguese court, led an expedition which sailed round the world in the Spanish interest, the first people ever to do so; he himself died on the way. In 1497 John Cabot sailed from Bristol and reached Newfoundland; the English pioneering was followed by Portugal, France and Holland. It will be obvious how these voyages enlarged the horizons of the old world and how much scope they gave to expanding trade.

# NATIONALISM

One thing stands out from this story. We find Portugal, Spain, England, France, Holland as prime agents. This is precisely what the Roman empire, the Holy Roman Empire, and the Catholic Church stood to avoid. There was a new force in the world, the force of nationalism. It arose for three reasons. Partly it was a relic of the past. The Roman empire had been broken by disunited barbarian tribes, which had settled in different areas which they made their own. Only the genius of Charlemagne had held them together at any time. The disunity was already there. Partly the new economic expansion led to rivalry between merchants from different towns or different areas, who invoked the support of their local king, prince or lord. Partly the new contact with Greece led people to think in terms of a political unit small enough for the individual to matter: only for the moment it was the educated individual of the upper or middle class only, and so the unit was the nation and not only the city-state of Plato or Aristotle, though this last had some parallel in Italy.


## THE REFORMATION

There remained the Christian Church. But the Church itself was corrupt. Its structure of authority reflected the pattern of feudal society; the new forces of individualism and nationalism challenged it, that is to say that 'each for himself' and 'each nation for itself' did not fit with the old order; the middle class did not find their religious needs satisfied. The new contact with Greece led to a new spirit of questioning.

The revolt—for the so-called Reformation was really a revolt—was led by a monk named Martin Luther (1483–1546). He was a man of deep sincerity and tumultuous energy. His protest against the corruptions of the Church was mixed with the desire of the Germans not to be ruled from Italy; for himself it came from the conviction of truth. His own words were 'Here I stand; I cannot do otherwise.' Luther was a product of the new individualism. He was wrestling with the problem of how he himself could be saved—not, he felt certain, by the word of the pope, nor by his own good works, but by the generosity of God, which men have only to accept. This is what he meant when he spoke of 'justification by faith'. Luther was excommunicated for his revolt, but he took with him many German Christians, and they founded a new Church, separate from the Catholics, abolishing many Catholic practices and using the German language in worship.

In England there was a similar desire to be rid of the rule of Rome. The occasion of the breakaway was a far less worthy one. The king, Henry VIII (b. 1491, ruled 1509–47), wanted to divorce his first wife and marry again; the pope would not permit this, and the king refused to obey the pope. From

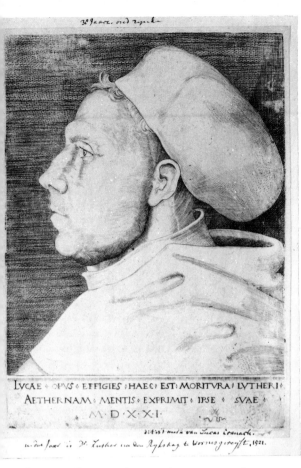

MARTIN LUTHER in 1521, from an engraving
by Lucas Cranach. Luther is still wearing the
habit of a monk.

CALVIN as a young man.

this unpromising start was born the Church of England, and an archbishop
of Canterbury, who was weak in his dealings with Henry but of sincere
devotion and possessing a fine command of words, Thomas Cranmer (1489–
1556) gave it in the English language a prayer-book of rare beauty.

At Geneva in modern Switzerland the break from Rome is associated with
John Calvin (1509–64), a rigidly logical thinker who believed that God has
*predestined*—ordered beforehand—the fate of each man. For the elect, the
chosen, this was good news indeed, and Calvin's favourite text was 'If God
be for us, who can be against us?' But whereas in England and Germany the
Church tended to become subject to the state, Calvin believed that God
worked through his chosen few to build his holy commonwealth, and himself
ruled Geneva as such a holy commonwealth.

161

The Catholic answer to all this was, in the movement known as the Counter-Reformation, to form groups of deeply committed Christians. The most famous of these, the Society of Jesus or the Jesuits, was started by Ignatius Loyola (*c.* 1491–1556), and played a great part in missionary work in the newly discovered parts of the world.

The result of the Reformation was the break-up of the one Church into a multitude of sects. But it also brought a deepening of religious belief and practice, and religion became again relevant to very many people to whom it had ceased to seem so. The balance between what was gained and what was lost is not easy to reckon.


# LITERATURE

One aspect of the new nationalisms was that they abandoned Latin as the common language of educated people. Dante wrote his prose works in Latin; poets still wrote in Latin exquisite songs of spring. But Latin was no longer a living language; it had ceased to grow; it could not cope with the new forces which were bursting out. So writers turned to their own local languages (often derived from Latin along different lines) and in so doing found new resources of expression. The movement began in Italy. We have seen that Dante used Italian in *The Divine Comedy*, but the real revolutionary was Petrarch (1304–74), whose influence was greater because he was such a good Latinist.

The south wind is coming back, bringing the fine season, and the flowers, and the grass, her sweet family, along with her. The swallow and the nightingale are making a stir, and the spring is turning white and red in every place.

There is a cheerful look on the meadows, and peace in the sky, and the sun is well pleased, I'm thinking, looking downward, and the air and the waters and the earth herself are full of love, and every beast is turning back looking for its mate.

And what is coming to me is great sighing and trouble, which herself is drawing out of my deep heart, herself that has taken the key of it up to Heaven.

And it is this way I am, that the singing birds, and the flowers of the earth, and the sweet ladies, with their grace and comeliness, are the like of a desert to me, and wild beasts astray in it.

*Zefiro torna.* Here is the new poetry of the vernacular, the local language, and the new mood, well caught by the Irish translator, in which the poet is first and foremost concerned not with the world outside, but with himself. Petrarch pointed the way for Angelo Poliziano (1454–94), another poet who wrote with ease in both Latin and Italian, the statesman Ludovico Ariosto (1474–1533), author of an epic *Orlando Furioso*, and a greater epic writer, Torquato Tasso (1544–95).

The impulse came from Italy, but in each country the liberation was felt. In France the dissolute priest François Villon (*c.* 1431–65) was followed by the exquisite courtier Pierre Ronsard (1524–85). In prose we find the coarse, robust, scholarly, massive satire of François Rabelais (*c.* 1483–1553) and the precise, elegant and humane Michel de Montaigne (1533–92). In England Geoffrey Chaucer (*c.* 1340–1400) is the first great vernacular poet; the characters of his *Canterbury Tales* live today. The early sixteenth century saw such attractive poets of noble birth as Sir Thomas Wyatt (*c.* 1503–42) and the Earl of Surrey (*c.* 1517–47). Royalty itself engaged in verses. King Henry VIII (b. 1491, ruled 1509–47) was an accomplished poet and musician, and his daughter Elizabeth (b. 1533, ruled 1558–1603) took after him. Her reign was the climax of English poetry. Such figures as the gallant knight Sir Philip Sidney (1554–86) and the humbler but talented Edmund Spenser (*c.* 1552–99), with many others, point forward to the towering and unequalled genius of William Shakespeare (1564–1616).

This remarkable outburst of writing of high quality was further encouraged by the invention of printing from movable types; this is usually attributed to Gutenberg, but Coster of Haarlem has an equal claim; both were experimenting in the 1430s and 1440s. This was used to spread the classical literature from which the Renaissance took fire, and the knowledge of the Bible which was in itself a cause of the Reformation; later, to publish the new literature.


## ART

As in writing, so in painting the impulse came from Italy; here the Renaissance was born and from here it spread. The great centre in Italy was Florence. Here, as in literature, we find a person who anticipates the Renaissance, Giotto (1267–1336), a daring revolutionary, whose paintings of Francis of Assisi are among his best-loved. But Giotto was ahead of his time.

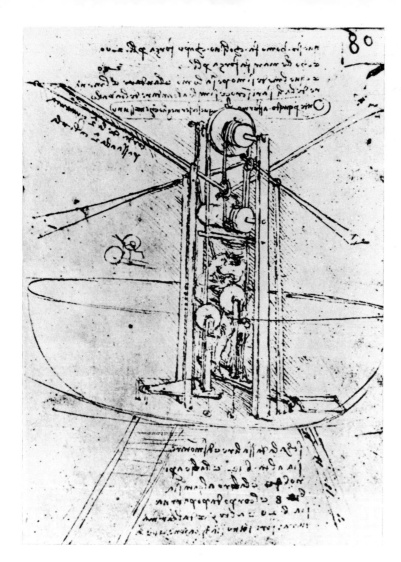

One of Leonardo da Vinci's designs for flying-machine. The man in the centre turns a handle, which through a system of gears makes the oar-like propeller blades revolve rather like a hand-driven helicopter.

Note that Leonardo, being left-handed wrote from right to left.

When the Renaissance came it meant the turning of the attention of painters from God to man. The highest point of artistic creation was reached by three contemporaries. Leonardo da Vinci (1452–1519) is one of the most remarkable all-round geniuses ever known. He was painter, sculptor, engineer, architect and inventor in a torrent of creative energy, the type of the many-sidedness of Renaissance man. He even devised a kind of flying-machine. The way in which he closely observed the movements of a running horse or the details of the human body show an artist whose interest lies on earth not in heaven. *The Last Supper*, which he painted for a church near Milan, set new standards in grouping figures in a picture. The famous *Mona Lisa*, now

MICHELANGELO: the dying slave. Notice that the slave's right foot seems still sunk in the block of marble on which he stands, and that the right leg is barely detached from the rough-hewn marble behind. There is a strong contrast between the highly polished limbs of the finished figure, and this remnant of the material from which the figure was carved. It is a reminder of the original great block from which the artist has created his vision of the completed form.

in Paris, shows a portrait painted by an artist who is fascinated by people. Raphael (1483–1520) is less original, but he sums up with his superb technique many of the tendencies of the Renaissance; he is famous for his pictures of the Mother and Child, Jesus with Mary. But there is no effort to create awe. Mary is a sweet and human mother, and Jesus a human child. Michelangelo (1475–1564), painter and sculptor, is thought by many the greatest of the three. He was a deeply religious man, whose interest in art centred largely upon the human body. As with the musician Beethoven and the dramatist Shakespeare, so with him you feel that art is trying to convey tremendous ideas with limited means, just as the slaves he carved seem to be bursting from the rocks which imprison them.

# FLORENCE

It will be noted that Florence was the key-point for the Renaissance. The reason was in part that in Italy the merchants had shut themselves up against the forces of popes and emperors in walled towns. In these limited communities a civilization not unlike that of Athens could develop. Commerce prospered and gave freedom for culture. An enlightened family of unofficial dictators, the Medicis, encouraged art and literature. The attitude of the times is seen in the writings of Niccolo Machiavelli (1469–1527). 'Machiavellian' has come to bear the meaning of 'unscrupulous', but this is unfair to Machiavelli. Machiavelli was a cold, hard realist, and though he lacked the high ideals of many founders of the Renaissance he was typical of them in that his eyes were fixed upon what works in this world. His most famous book, *The Prince*, is an attempt to show what works in politics.

# SCIENCE

A further result of the new economic order, the new concern with this world and the new spirit of inquiry was an impulse to science. In the later Middle Ages the science of the past was accepted on the authority of the past. If an observed fact conflicted with Aristotle, Galen (in medicine) or Ptolemy (in astronomy), it was assumed that the observation, not Aristotle, Galen or Ptolemy, was wrong. Now the authority of the Greeks was broken by the Greeks. In 1543 was published (by the new printing) a translation of

The three great inventions which changed the face of the world were the compass, the printing press, and gunpowder.

The mariner's compass enabled sailors to move confidently out of sight of land. It came into use in about the twelfth century. At first it consisted of a magnetized needle thrust through a straw and floated by it on the surface of water in a bowl. The next step was to attach to the needle a card showing the 'points' and to support the whole element on a central pivot in a bowl, usually of wood. This illustration of a compass made in 1719 shows a type which remained basically unchanged from about 1300 until well into the nineteenth century.

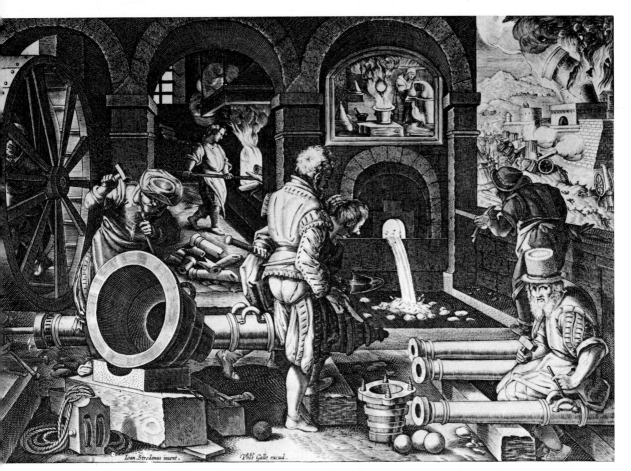

A sixteenth-century gun-foundry. Molten gun-metal is pouring from the furnace into a prepared mould. The treadmill on the left turns the tool which bores out the barrel. In the foreground men with chisels are giving the finishing touches. The wide-mouthed weapon is a mortar. Two little scenes let into the picture show the legendary medieval discoverer of gunpowder, the monk Berthold Schwarz of Germany, and a contemporary scene of siege, with guns battering down stone defences.

Archimedes, and experimental science began. Nicolaus Copernicus (1473–1543) is often called the founder of modern science; but though he put forward the view that the sun, not the earth, is at the centre of what we now call the solar system, he was in general conservative, dogmatic and arbitrary, and observed very little himself. More important, and a true product of the new age, was the Dane Tycho Brahe (1546–1601), a splendid observer, in whose honour the future King James I of England (then king of Scotland) wrote a poem. His work really does point to modern science. The new spirit is summed up by Francis Bacon (1561–1628), a weak and corrupt politician,

A sixteenth-century printing house, with two wooden presses. On the left compositors are taking types from the cases, and setting them in composing-'sticks'. On the right one pressman is pulling the bar of his press, bringing paper and inked type together under pressure. Behind him a second pressman is rubbing ink-balls on the type, ready for the next impression. Between the presses printed sheets are hanging up to dry.

THE 'GUTENBERG' BIBLE, almost certainly the first book printed in Europe from movable types. The facts are not entirely certain, but it is highly likely that this book was printed in Mainz, in Germany, in about 1455. It gives the Vulgate text (St Jerome's Latin translation) of the Bible. Perhaps 240 copies were printed on paper and 30 on vellum (calf-skin). This is a vellum copy, now in Lambeth Palace library. Copies on vellum would be for rich buyers, and were richly decorated. The border of leaves was painted in by hand after printing. So were the lines in red. Compare the manuscript shown earlier in this book: the printed book looks very like them in some ways. But in about thirty years the printer had learnt to do without hand-written decoration and headings, and by 1550 books looked very much more like those of today. But roman type took a long time to replace the old 'black-letter' based on medieval handwriting. In England black-letter ceased to be used in the seventeenth century. In Germany black-letter was still being used in this century.

utiq; sequeremur si antea cognouisse-
mus . Sic aut vos de gentis nobili-
tate iactatis : quasi no moru imitato
magis q carnalis natiuitas filios
vos faciat esse sanctoru. Deniq; esau
z rsmahel cu de stirpe sint abrate : mini-
me tamen in filios reputant. Hijs ta-
liter altercantibz-apostolus se mediu
interponens : ita partiu dirimit questi-
ones-ut neutru eox sua iusticia salute
meruisse cofirmet : ambos vero ipsos
et scienter z grauiter deliquisse : iudeos
qp per puaricatione legis deu inpro-
rauerunt : gentes vero qp cu cognitu de
creatura creatorem ut deu debuerit ve-
netari-gloria eius in manufacta mu-
tauerint simulacra : vtrosq; etia simili-
ter venia cosecutos · equales esse vera-
rissima ratione demonstrat : psertim
rium in eade lege pdictum z iudeos et
gentes ad cristi fidem vocandos esse
ostender . Quamobrem vicissim eos
humilians : ad pacem et concordi-
am cohortatur Explicit plogus spe-
nalis Incipit plogus tercius.

Omani sut partis ytalie.
Qij pueniti sunt a falsis
apostolis : z sub nomine
dni nostri ihesu cristi in le-
gem z pphetas erant induci. Hos re-
vocat apsus ad vera z euagelica fide
scribens ei a corintp Explicit plogus
Incipit epla ad Romanos

Aulus seruus ihesu
cristi-vocat9 apsus
segregatus in euan-
geliu dei-qd ate pro-
miserat per pphetas
suos i scripturis san-
ctis de filio suo · qui factus9 e ei ex semi-
ne dauid scdm carne : qui pdestinat9
est filius dei in virtute scdm spiritu

sanctificationis ex resurrectione mor-
tuox ihesu cristi dni nri: p que accepi-
mus gratia et apostolatu ad obedie-
dum fidei in omnibz gentibus pro nomine eius:in quibz estis z vos vocati
ihesu cristi : omnibus qui sunt rome-
dilectis dei vocatis sanctis. Gratia vobis z pax a deo patre z dno nro ihesu
cristo . Primu quide gratas ago do
meo per ihesu cristu pro omnibz vobis:
quia fides vra annuciatur in vniuer-
so mudo . Testis enim mihi est deus
cui seruio in spiritu meo in euangelio
filij eius: qp sine intermissione memori-
am vestri facio semp in orationibus
meis : obsecrans si quo modo tande
aliquando psperu iter habea in volu-
tate dei veniendi ad vos. Desidero eni
videre vos : ut aliquid impertiar vobis gratie spiritualis ad confirmados
vos: id est simul consolari in vobis
per eam que inuicem est fidem vestra
atq; meam. Nolo aut vos ignorare
fratres : qa sepe pposui venire ad vos
et phibit9 sum usq; adhuc: ut alique
fructu habea in vobis sicut z in ceteris
gentibus. Grecis ac barbaris sapienti-
bus z insipientibz debitor sum: itaq;
qd in me, pmptu e et vobis qui rome
estis euangelizare. No enim erubesco
euangeliu. Virtus eni dei est in salute
omni credenti: iudeo primu et greco.
Iusticia enim dei i eo reuelatur ex fide
in fidem : sicut scriptu est. Just9 autem
ex fide viuit. Reuelatur enim ira dei de
celo sup omne impietate et iniusticia
hominu : eox qui veritate dei i iniusticia detinet: qa qd notu e dei manifestu
est i illis. Deus eni illis reuelauit. In-
uisibilia eni ipse9 a creatura mudi per
ea q facta sut intellecta cospiciunt: sem-
piterna quoq; eius virt9 et diuinitas:

but a great teacher of scientific method, who insisted that knowledge will grow from looking at the world, not from reading books, and that experiment is the basis of scientific method. He who seeks knowledge should first look at things which happen in the world around; he should then ask himself what causes them to happen; and, having formed a theory, he should experiment to see whether that cause does in fact produce that result. This is the method of modern science.

## HUMANISM

It will be clear that one of the chief effects of the Renaissance was to turn attention from God to man. The reason for this was partly the break-up of the old economic order in which each was a member of a community and its replacement by an order in which each was out for himself, partly the new learning which brought an interest in classical as well as Christian themes and which encouraged the attitude of the Greeks themselves, partly the bursting of the bounds of the old world in new interests and new knowledge. The result can be seen in many places. Christian people themselves are concerned with their own salvation rather than the glory of God. Artists turn from picturing religious scenes in order to stir up reverence, to painting or sculpting human beings. Machiavelli writes not of what God commands but of what humans can do. Poets are interested in their own thoughts and their own emotions. The mood of the Renaissance is well expressed in some words from Shakespeare's *Hamlet*:

What a piece of work is a man! How noble in reason! how infinite in faculties! in form and moving, how express and admirable! in action, how like an angel! in apprehension, how like a God!—the beauty of the world! the paragon of animals!

GIULIANO DE' MEDICI (d. 1516), as represented by Michelangelo in the Medici Chapel at Florence. Michelangelo saw Giuliano as a symbol of the life of activity; the turn of the head, the slanting line of the hands and baton, the position of the knees and feet suggest keen awareness, and stern self-command which can at any minute turn to action: the figure is poised to rise to its feet. Giuliano is wearing the closely moulded armour of a Roman general of classical times and indeed it is so closely modelled on the forms of the body that he seems part-naked. This enables Michelangelo to suggest an immensely powerful athletic body—though the face is youthful. The citizens of Florence pointed out that there was no resemblance to the Giuliano they had known. Michelangelo retorted that in a thousand years no one would know or care what the real Giuliano had looked like. He knew that the vitality of his symbolic figure would be as powerful in 2534 as it was in 1534: it represents the Renaissance ideals of manly activity, nobility, self-confidence, physical beauty.

# II

# THE PAST IN THE PRESENT

## FROM THE RENAISSANCE TO THE PRESENT DAY

THE Renaissance is the link between the old world and the new. It set man off on a fresh start. The civilization which sprang from the Renaissance grew throughout western Europe; it spread to the Americas, to many parts of Africa, and to the South Seas. It affected India, Japan and China. Russia, less touched than western Europe, inherited Byzantine Christianity on one side, became linked with western science, literature and art on the other side, and in this century has been profoundly affected by Karl Marx, who in his moral fervour was a descendant of the Hebrew prophets, and stands in a line of political thinkers which can be traced back to Greece. Meantime, the influence of Islam, which itself was affected by Greece and Palestine, remains strongest in North Africa, the Near East, some parts of central Asia, and Pakistan. There is almost no part of the civilized world which can be understood without a knowledge of the world of the Mediterranean in ancient times. The old civilizations of China and India, fascinating and glorious as they are, have never spread their influence widely outside those countries. But we are all heirs of the Mediterranean world.

From 1910 the western world has been cracking. A disastrous war in Europe from 1914 to 1918 was followed by ten uneasy years. Then came economic crisis, and the emergence of new forms of tyranny, and ten years later the still more disastrous war of 1939–45. Meantime the stupendous advance of physical science has left untold possibilities for good or evil. Travelling to the moon has become a real prospect; so has the self-destruction of mankind. We are in a period of transition; it is the more important that we shall look at the past and see how society has grown to the present, that we shall examine the values we have inherited and see which are good and useful and which are not. We should not let ourselves be the object of the epigram that the only lesson to be learned from history is that nobody ever learns anything from history.

## LANGUAGE

One of the places where we can most obviously see the past in the present is in the very words we use. In the United Nations there are five world-languages—English, French, Spanish, Russian and Chinese. The first three of these are largely derived from Latin, as also are Italian, Portuguese and Rumanian. In the first section of this chapter the words *Renaissance, civilization, science, literature, art, century, possibilities, important, present*, to name but a few, come from Latin; so do *section* and *chapter*. Words teach us to think, and in this way our thoughts unite us with those who have gone before. Greek is the language of science, and there are not many scientific words which do not come from the Greek. Examples of words with a Greek origin are: *physics, mathematics, arithmetic, geometry, biology, zoology, atom, electron, energy*. There are many others.

## RELIGION

Let us look next at man's highest aspirations. We have seen that, from the first, primitive man believed himself to be living in a *supernatural* as well as a *natural* world. In the primitive stage this belief is mixed up with magic and superstition and often leads to practices which civilized man regards as cruel. Most, though not all, of those civilized people who believe that religion matters, see a belief in one god (monotheism) as something higher than a belief in many gods (polytheism), and think that a man's religion ought to lead to higher standards in his behaviour towards other people. These two aspects, monotheism and morality, are shown supremely in the three world-religions which have come to us from the Mediterranean area—Judaism, Christianity and Islam. All three are living forces in the twentieth century.

## PHILOSOPHY

When Thales asked his question about the world in which we live, he was starting something new. One question led to another, and the stream of philosophy is continuous from Thales to the present day. It is generally acknowledged that Plato and Aristotle are among the most outstanding figures in the history of philosophy, and anyone who wants to think about problems which are still important today might do worse than start from them. In a 900-page book entitled *The History of Western Philosophy* Bertrand Russell gives 300 pages to the Greeks and a further 200 to the period separating the Greeks from the Renaissance. Even those modern thinkers who believe that philosophy should confine itself to the analysis of language have found that Plato anticipates many of their discussions.


## SCIENCE AND MATHEMATICS

It might seem that science has advanced so far since ancient times that there is no need to bother with what the ancient world thought. This would be a mistake.

In the first place the Greeks in particular had the scientific attitude to a marked degree. They had an insatiable curiosity combined with a refusal to accept slipshod or superstitious answers. We can today still 'catch' this attitude from the Greeks. We do well to remember that it was a translation of Archimedes which inspired the beginning of modern science.

Secondly, the sheer achievement in mathematics is astonishing. The great mathematician G. H. Hardy wrote 'Oriental mathematics may be an interesting curiosity, but Greek mathematics is the real thing', and his friend and colleague Littlewood said 'The Greeks are not clever schoolboys or scholarship candidates but fellows at another college.' We have seen that Euclid was until recent years a standard text-book in geometry; we know that one of the most famous theorems still bears the name of Pythagoras. Add to this the contribution of the Arabs when they devised a symbol for 0, and remember that the very word 'algebra' is Arabic, and something of our debt to the ancients becomes plain.

Thirdly, even in things scientific the past shines within the present. The typical plan of a modern town in America, or some of the new towns in Africa, is that of the Hellenistic towns. A recent history-book shows a block of flats in ancient Rome compared with a block of flats in modern London; it is not easy to decide at a glance which is which. Or again the Greek doctor took an oath in which he promised to maintain the highest standards of integrity in his profession, the so-called Hippocratic oath, and Charles Singer, the historian of science, could write: 'Respected equally throughout the ages by Arab, Jew and Christian, the oath remains the watchword of the profession of medicine.'

## MUSIC

We do not know much about the music of the ancient world, and it has not had much effect upon modern music. It might therefore seem strange to include music as a field in which we can see the past living in the present. Yet it is right to do so, for two reasons.

First, modern music derives from the worship of the Christian Church in the Middle Ages. We have seen how Pliny found the Christians singing a hymn to Christ as God. For many reasons much of the worship of the Christian Church was chanted—it was easier to remember, clearer to hear, and added to the beauty of the service. This was developed after the Renaissance, and found its highest point in the work of Johann Sebastian Bach (1685–1750). Secular, that is non-church, music was derived from church music, and long followed the same pattern. Some of the greatest music of the twentieth century has been written for religious use; we may mention Edward Elgar's *The Dream of Gerontius*, William Walton's massive *Belshazzar's Feast*, the Hungarian Kodaly's *Missa Brevis*, or the setting of the *Mass* by Igor Stravinsky (b. 1882), who holds the same sort of position in music that Picasso does in painting.

Secondly, we often find that although the music does not in any real sense go back to the ancient world, the theme of the music does. Stravinsky, for example, wrote an opera *Oedipus Rex* based on a play of Sophocles. Carl Orff (b. 1895), a German composer, set in wonderfully exciting rhythms some poems by the Roman poet Catullus and some medieval Latin lyrics. A more important German composer, Richard Strauss (1864–1949), wrote operas on classical themes. Jean Sibelius (1865–1958), the great composer from Finland, who often evokes the northern forests in his music, has confessed that ancient Greece exercised a strong influence on his musical thinking. Ralph Vaughan Williams, who did much for English religious music—many have

sung his tunes to 'For all the saints' and 'Come down, O Love Divine'—
wrote the music for a performance of a comedy *The Wasps* by the ancient
Greek Aristophanes.


## ART

Until the end of the nineteenth century European art was derived in a
direct line from the Greeks, with very little outside influence. Then some
artists became fascinated by Japanese colour-prints and others by African
Negro sculpture. The break-up of the order of European life in two world wars
and the depression in between has led to a break-up of artistic values and the
creation of broken, distorted images. But the old values are not lost. The
tension can be seen in the most original genius of the time, Pablo Picasso
(b. 1881), who sometimes draws harsh crude figures and sometimes classical
heads derived directly from the Greek. The break-up of society has made art
unstable; the continuing inspiration of Greece has kept a thread of stability.
Young artists from Africa and elsewhere are combining the traditions of their
own parts of the world with the sense of balance and beauty they derive from
contact with Greece.


## LITERATURE

When we come to literature we find the same story. Outstanding contemporary poets have set themselves to translate works of literature from Greece
and Rome. Thus Rex Warner, Louis MacNeice, Richard Lattimore and
Patric Dickinson have translated Greek plays; Cecil Day Lewis has rendered
in English most of the works of Vergil; Robert Graves has issued versions of
Apuleius and Suetonius. W. B. Yeats (1865–1939), the Irish writer, found his
inspiration in Byzantium. The most familiar of modern writers, T. S. Eliot
(b. 1888), has in each of his plays (with one exception) taken a Greek original;
his verses are full of references to classical myths and lines from ancient
authors.

> Paint me a cavernous waste shore
>   Cast in the unstilled Cyclades,
> Paint me the bold anfractuous rocks
>   Faced by the snarled and yelping seas.

A flute-player, by Picasso, showing how the artist has added to the long tradition of pastoral art, which stretches back in literature, art and music to the ancient Greeks. A shepherd, his head crowned with a wreath of laurel or vine leaves, plays to a shepherdess holding a tambourine.

In his most famous poem *The Waste Land* he uses the mythical figures of the blind prophet Tiresias and the nightingale Philomela, and quotes the Roman poet Ovid, a late Latin poem *The Vigil of Venus,* and the *Confessions* of Augustine.

Perhaps the most important movement in recent literature has been the revival of drama in France. Jean Giraudoux (1882–1944) is the leading playwright of the period. He took Greek (and also Biblical) themes and presented them in modern terms. Thus, when he wanted to show the futility of war he took the old story of the conflict between Greeks and Trojans and wrote *The Trojan War Will not Take Place.* He was followed by Jean Cocteau (b. 1889), Jean-Paul Sartre (b. 1905) and Jean Anouilh (b. 1910). Each of these has found that the Greeks have presented the problem or theme with which he is concerned. This is most remarkable in Anouilh's *Antigone* where he found, in France under German occupation, that the old Greek story which Sophocles had shown on the stage expressed the clash between the individual and the state which he wanted to write about.

## POLITICS

The German poet Goethe once said 'Mankind advances, but man remains the same'. The political problems of the modern world are not essentially different from those of the ancient world, where we can study them and see them more clearly, on a smaller scale, interpreted by men of genius. In 1948 there was a civil war in Greece. A masterly analysis of that conflict is given by the historian Thucydides, writing nearly twenty-four centuries before it took place:

Revolution thus ran its course from city to city, and the places which it arrived at last, from having heard what had been done before, carried to a still greater excess the refinement of their inventions, as shown in the cunning of their enterprises and the atrocity of their reprisals. Words had to change their ordinary meaning. Reckless audacity became staunch courage; prudent hesitation, specious cowardice; moderation was held to be a cloak for unmanliness; ability to see all sides inability to act on any.... The advocate of extreme measures was always trustworthy; his opponent a man to be suspected. Blood became a weaker tie than party, from the superior readiness of the latter to dare everything without reserve.... The leaders in the cities, each provided with the fairest professions, on the one side with the cry of political equality of the people, on

178

the other of an ordered aristocracy, sought prizes for themselves in those public interests which they pretended to cherish, and, recoiling from no means in their struggle for ascendancy, dared and went through with the direst excesses, which were met in their turn by reprisals still more terrible....Religion was in honour with neither party, but the use of fair names to arrive at guilty ends was in high reputation. Meanwhile the moderate part of the citizens perished between the two, either for not joining in the quarrel, or because envy would not suffer them to escape.

Our political institutions can be traced back to the Greeks, with the important difference that we practise *representative* government where they normally practised *direct* government. The arguments in favour of different forms of government, democracy, oligarchy and monarchy, are stated once and for all in the pages of the historian Herodotus or the philosophers Plato and Aristotle. We can see how democracy at Athens inspired the people but proved unstable, or how monarchy at Rome gave stability, peace and prosperity, but failed to give people the will to do things for themselves.

The great political problem of our time is to make different peoples conscious that they are citizens of one world. Alexander had this vision, but did not live to fulfil it. The Romans proved more successful here than anyone else before or since; the Holy Roman Empire was an attempt to recapture the unity that had been lost. The United Nations can still learn from the Romans.

The headquarters of the United Nations and the Manhattan skyline, seen from the East River, New York. The tall rectangular building is the secretariat; the building with the upward-curving roof and dome houses the council chambers and conference rooms.

# LAW

We have seen how Hammurabi at Babylon was responsible for one of the first great legal codes, and how some of his ideas passed into Jewish and so into Christian and Islamic thought. Meantime the Athenian democracy, lacking stability, found it in the rule of law, which might prevent the Assembly from acting with complete irresponsibility. Socrates, in prison and condemned to death, had the opportunity of escaping. He refused. He said that he had lived his life under the protection of the laws; he had accepted their verdict when it was in his favour, and he would not try to evade it now that it was not in his favour.

But the greatest contribution to Law was made by the Romans. Their first code, the Twelve Tables, no doubt owed something to Greece, but from there they developed along their own lines. Under the early empire important advances were made, and the Stoics introduced a distinction between the law of the country (*ius civile*) and the law of nature (*ius naturae*), which corresponds crudely to what is legally right and what is morally right, and which influenced the development of *equity* alongside that of *law*. These advances were put together in the codes of Justinian, and the rediscovery of these was a major factor in the development of law in western Europe and those parts of the world in contact with western Europe; this applies to the U.S.A., for example, or to the emergent nations of Africa. Here, in the field of law, if anywhere, the past may be said to live in the present.

# HUMAN RIGHTS

A practical example of the importance of the past for the present may be seen in the Universal Declaration of Human Rights which passed the United Nations Assembly on 10 December 1948. Here was an attempt to achieve international co-operation in promoting and encouraging respect for human rights and fundamental freedoms for all without distinction as to race, sex, language or religion, according to the United Nations Charter. Here was a document which had to find acceptance throughout the world, and it is remarkable how many of its clauses owe their origin to those parts of the ancient world which this book has been studying. For example, the idea of the brotherhood of man goes back to Alexander, the Stoics and the New

Testament. The emphasis on law can be traced to Deuteronomy, Plato, the Romans and Byzantium. The emphasis on the freedom of family comes from the Old Testament, on freedom of thought from Socrates, Luther and the Renaissance. Social security, which has been much developed in the last hundred years, still owes something to Plato, the Middle Ages, and some Renaissance writers. Education is fundamental in Plato (who in his last book suggested that the Minister of Education should be Prime Minister) and Aristotle, and also in Islam. The demand for a social and international order in which these rights can be realized belongs to the Romans and to the Catholic Church. The insistence that duties exist alongside rights is found in Plato and the Stoics, as well as the Middle Ages.

## CONCLUSION

Here then we see the reasons for our study of the ancient world.

First, we see there the roots from which our own world has grown. We cannot understand the modern world without knowing something about the ancients.

Secondly, precisely because of this direct line of succession, we can study many of our own problems in the ancient world more clearly and objectively, and learn from their errors and successes.

Thirdly, we see in the ancient world some of the highest achievements of man. We shall not achieve great things ourselves by merely copying them. But if we study and understand our predecessors we may be inspired as they were inspired. The world owes an incalculable debt to the religious genius of Judaism, Christianity and Islam, the artistic, literary and philosophical genius of the Greeks which was revived at the Renaissance, and the practical genius of the Romans.

# FOR FURTHER READING

The books which follow are not necessarily the main authorities on the subject, but are all interesting and readable for anyone who wishes to follow up particular periods or aspects. They include some novels.

## CHAPTER I

A. C. B. Lovell, *The Individual and the Universe.*
F. Hoyle, *The Nature of the Universe.*
J. Jeans, *The Mysterious Universe.*
V. Gordon Childe, *What Happened in History.*
H. Peake and H. J. Fleure, *The Corridors of Time.*
L. Cottrell, *The Lost Pharaohs.*
—— *Life under the Pharaohs.*

L. Cottrell, *The Bull of Minos.*
M. Murray, *The Splendour that was Egypt.*
L. Woolley, *Ur of the Chaldees.*
Mary Renault, *The King Must Die.*
J. H. Breasted, *Ancient Times.*
Arnold Toynbee, *A Study of History* (abridged by D. C. Somervell).
T. R. Glover, *The Ancient World.*

## CHAPTER 2

The Old Testament.
W. O. E. Oesterley and T. H. Robinson, *Hebrew Religion.*
H. W. Robinson, *The Religious Ideas of the Old Testament.*

N. H. Snaith, *The Distinctive Ideas of the Old Testament.*
E. W. Heaton, *The Old Testament Prophets.*
H. W. Robinson, *The History of Israel.*
W. A. L. Elmslie, *How Came Our Faith.*

## CHAPTER 3

H. D. F. Kitto, *The Greeks.*
G. L. Dickinson, *The Greek View of Life.*
R. W. Livingstone, *The Greek Genius and its Meaning to Us.*
—— (ed.), *The Legacy of Greece.*
F. R. Earp, *The Way of the Greeks.*
A. E. Zimmern, *The Greek Commonwealth.*
W. K. C. Guthrie, *The Greek Philosophers.*
Homer, *Iliad*, tr. E. V. Rieu.

Thucydides, *The Peloponnesian War*, tr. R. W. Livingstone.
Plato, *The Republic*, tr. F. M. Cornford.
Aristotle, Selections, tr. W. D. Ross.
R. Lattimore (ed.), *The Complete Greek Drama.*
Naomi Mitchison, *Cloud-Cuckoo Land.*
Mary Renault, *The Last of the Wine.*

## CHAPTER 4

W. W. Tarn and G. T. Griffith, *Hellenistic Civilization.*
W. W. Tarn, *Alexander the Great.*
E. R. Bevan, *Stoics and Sceptics.*

A. J. Festugière, *Epicurus and his Gods.*
B. Farrington, *Greek Science.*
Naomi Mitchison, *The Corn King and Spring Queen.*

182

## CHAPTER 5

W. W. Fowler and M. P. Charlesworth, *Rome.*
M. P. Charlesworth, *The Roman Empire.*
C. Bailey (ed.), *The Legacy of Rome.*
J. Buchan, *Augustus.*
J. Carcopino, *Daily Life in Ancient Rome.*
H. J. Haskell, *This was Cicero.*
M. Grant, *Roman Readings.*
Vergil, *Aeneid*, tr. C. Day Lewis.

Horace, *Odes*, tr. E. Marsh.
Tacitus, *On Imperial Rome*, tr. M. Grant.
Naomi Mitchison, *The Conquered.*
R. Graves, *I Claudius.*
—— *Claudius the God.*
E. B. Lytton, *The Last Days of Pompeii.*
M. Yourcenar, *Memoirs of Hadrian.*
W. Pater, *Marius the Epicurean.*

## CHAPTER 6

The New Testament.
T. R. Glover, *The Jesus of History.*
A. S. Peake and R. F. Parsons, *An Outline of Christianity.*

G. B. Caird, *The Apostolic Age.*
E. R. Bevan, *Christianity.*
Saint Augustine, *Confessions*, tr. F. J. Sheed.
Naomi Mitchison, *The Blood of the Martyrs.*

## CHAPTER 7

S. Runciman, *Byzantine Civilization.*
N. H. Baynes, *The Byzantine Empire.*
N. H. Baynes and H. St L. B. Moss, *Byzantium.*

D. Talbot Rice, *Byzantine Art.*
Joan M. Hussey, *The Byzantine World.*
C. Diehl, *Byzantine Portraits.*
R. Graves, *Count Belisarius.*

## CHAPTER 8

The Quran.
T. Arnold and A. Guillaume (eds.), *The Legacy of Islam.*
A. Guillaume, *Islam.*

E. Dermenghem, *Muhammad.*
A. J. Arberry, *Sufism.*
M. Smith (ed.), *Readings from the Mystics of Islam.*

## CHAPTER 9

C. W. Previté-Orton, *The Shorter Cambridge Medieval History.*
G. G. Coulton, *Medieval Panorama.*
—— *The Medieval Scene.*
E. K. Rand, *Founders of the Middle Ages.*
N. Pevsner, *An Outline of European Architecture.*
Helen Waddell (ed.), *Medieval Latin Lyrics.*

J. B. Ross and M. M. McLaughlin (eds.), *The Portable Medieval Reader.*
C. G. Crump and E. F. Jacob (eds.), *The Legacy of the Middle Ages.*
Dante, *The New Life*, tr. D. G. Rossetti.
—— *The Divine Comedy*, parts I, II, tr. Dorothy L. Sayers.
Helen Waddell, *Peter Abelard.*

## CHAPTER 10

J. K. Huizinga, *The Waning of the Middle Ages.*
R. H. Tawney, *Religion and the Rise of Capitalism.*
R. H. Bainton, *The Reformation of the Sixteenth Century.*
—— *Here I Stand.*
Erasmus, *In Praise of Folly.*

B. Berenson, *Italian Painters of the Renaissance.*
H. Butterfield, *The Origins of Modern Science.*
W. Shakespeare, *Plays.*
N. Ault (ed.), *Elizabethan Lyrics.*
J. Burckhardt, *The Civilization of the Renaissance in Italy.*

## CHAPTER II

Stringfellow Barr, *The Pilgrimage of Western Man.*
Bertrand Russell, *History of Western Philosophy.*

G. Highet, *The Classical Tradition.*
W. G. de Burgh, *The Legacy of the Ancient World.*

# ACKNOWLEDGMENTS

Thanks are due to the following for permission to reproduce the plates in this book:

P. 2 British Museum (Natural History), Professor Grahame Clark; p. 3 the Mansell Collection; p. 6 Professor Grahame Clark; p. 8 Paul Popper; p. 9 Thames and Hudson Ltd and Director-General, Service des antiquités, Cairo; p. 10 British Museum; p. 11 and title-page, Thames and Hudson Ltd; p. 12 Archives photographiques, Paris; p. 13 Professor Grahame Clark; p. 14 Hirmer Verlag, Munich; p. 15 Professor Grahame Clark; p. 19 Mansell Collection (Alinari); p. 20 Matson Photo Service, Los Angeles; p. 22 Mansell Collection (Anderson); p. 24 Mansell Collection (Anderson); p. 25 American Schools of Oriental Research, New Haven, Conn.; p. 31 A. F. Kersting; p. 33 British Museum; p. 34 Danish National Museum; p. 39 J. Allan Cash; p. 40 Mansell Collection (Anderson); p. 43 Alison Frantz, Athens; p. 44 D. A. Harissiadis, Athens; pp. 45, 47 British Museum; p. 51 Mansell Collection (Alinari); p. 53 Museum, Istanbul; pp. 55, 60, 61, 66, 69, 70, 72 Mansell Collection (Anderson and Alinari); p. 73 Nuellens, Aachen; p. 76 Mansell Collection (Alinari); p. 77 Philipson Studios, Newcastle; p. 79 Mansell Collection (Anderson); p. 81 Kunsthistorisch Instituut, Nijmegen; p. 82 Comitato di Azione Patriottica, Rome; p. 82 Institute of Classical Studies; p. 86 Matson Photo Service; p. 87 Mansell Collection (Anderson); p. 90 Victoria and Albert Museum; p. 92 Mansell Collection (Anderson); p. 95 Uitgevers maatschappij Elsevier; p. 98 Mrs George Allan; p. 99 Mansell Collection (Alinari); p. 100 Mansell Collection (Alinari); p. 101 Mansell Collection (Anderson); pp. 106, 109 Mansell Collection (Anderson); p. 110 Paul Popper; p. 113 Lincoln College, Oxford; p. 117 Royal Asiatic Society; p. 117 A. F. Kersting; p. 119 Royal Geographical Society; p. 119 Paul Popper; p. 121 Francis Uher; p. 126 University Library, Cambridge; p. 131 Nuellens, Aachen; p. 133 Kunsthistorisches Museum, Vienna; pp. 135, 136 Bibliothèque Nationale, Paris; pp. 138, 139 Lala Aufsberg, Sonthofen im Allgäu; p. 140 Mansell Collection (Alinari); p. 142 Bibliothèque Nationale; pp. 144, 145 Umschau Verlag, Frankfurt; p. 146 A. F. Kersting; p. 146 Helga Schmidt-Glassner, Stuttgart; pp. 147, 148 A. F. Kersting; p. 149 J. Allan Cash; p. 152 Mansell Collection (Alinari); p. 157 A.C.L., Brussels; p. 158 Bibliothèque Nationale; p. 161 Rijksmuseum, Amsterdam; p. 161 Jean, Arland, Geneva; pp. 164, 165 Mansell Collection; p. 166 National Maritime Museum; p. 169 Lambeth Palace Library; p. 171 Mansell Collection; p. 177 S.P.A.D.E.M., Paris; p. 179 United Nations.